W0275133

JAMES BROWN & HELENA HUNT

WALKER STUDIO

CONTENTS

WHAT IS ART?

It is a difficult question to answer because art can be so many things. Humans have been making it for at least 70,000 years – and probably much, much longer – and throughout that time it has taken many different forms. That makes the world of art an enormous place to explore.

WHAT FORMS MIGHT ART TAKE? Music, plays, poetry, all of these things are considered to be art, but in this book we will be looking at visual art – art which takes a visible form first and foremost. It could be carved from stone, painted on a canvas, modelled from clay, or captured by a camera. Art can also be made using fireworks, light, your body, and objects you can find in your cupboard. It can be so small it fits in your pocket or so big it towers over you. It might look exactly like something or someone – or like nothing you've ever seen before. Throughout history artists have invented new methods of making art, and scientific discoveries have provided innovative ways for artists to create.

So, what makes something art when it can be made from so many things and look like almost anything? Art is a form of expression and communication. It shows us an idea, an emotion or a belief, and when we see it we often can't help but experience something. To explore and make it, an artist will usually use imagination, creativity and often some degree of skill.

What is the purpose of art, then? That's another big question. Art can give something meaning, send a message, tell a story, reflect something about ourselves and many other things besides. We can use it in a huge number of ways. Today we view artworks in museums and galleries, but in many cases that means we are viewing it outside of how it would originally have appeared. However, it can still teach us about different cultures' ways of life, how they saw the world and what they found important as, for thousands of years, most of art has had a function, often connected to religion, wealth or power. Forty thousand years ago, our ancestors who relied on hunting and gathering to stay alive spent precious time creating sculptures from mammoth ivory, at least one of which was used in a ritual. Rulers decorated buildings with images designed to show their subjects how powerful they were. Artworks were created for tombs for use in the afterlife and buried, meant never to be seen again by the living. But sometimes art is made just for the sake of making art.

Ideas about what art can be have evolved over time and it certainly isn't something everyone agrees on. What we might think of as art might never have been intended to be so at all; different cultures think of art in different ways – or not at all – and within the same culture there might be disagreement over what art is. Works have even gone to trial to prove they *are* art! One artist who questioned art was Marcel Duchamp. In 1917 he submitted a white porcelain urinal on its back, which he had signed with the name *R. Mutt* and called *Fountain*, to an exhibition. He was an artist, he called it art, and it was intended to be shown in an art exhibition setting. Does that make it art? He thought so. He had chosen something which was already made, changed the way we look at it, and given it a new meaning. It was a challenge to what art was traditionally thought to be and, although the exhibition rejected it, Duchamp's work was an important moment in thinking about how we view art.

From the earliest artworks to today's, art sparks something in us and requires a spark to make it. Throughout our history, art has been a vital part of who we are – and will continue to be long into our future.

CAVE PAINTING

Before we invented the wheel or had begun to read and write, we were making art. But it is only in the past 150 years that we have known about the first artists' creations. Of the art that has been discovered, paintings in caves are some of the most spectacular. Cave painting is a type of rock art, a tradition that has continued into the modern world.

IN NORTHERN SPAIN in 1879, a girl called Maria was exploring a cave with her father, amateur archaeologist Marcelino Sanz de Sautuola. The cave is called Altamira and Marcelino was looking for traces of the people who had lived there tens of thousands of years ago. The story goes that whilst they were investigating the cave, Maria looked up and spotted paintings of animals on the ceiling. What she and her father had found were works of art dating back between 36,000 and 23,000 years ago to a period known as the Paleolithic – the Old Stone Age.

Patterns made on stones found in South Africa dating back over 70,000 years are thought to be some of our earliest artworks.

Marcelino realized these paintings were Paleolithic, but initially many people thought they were modern forgeries. As more cave paintings were found, he was proved right, and Paleolithic works of art have now been found in caves and on rock surfaces in many countries, from Spain and France to Russia. The oldest painted scenes date back around 44,000 years and as archaeologists continue to make new discoveries, some paintings may well be found which are older still.

Cave paintings often depict similar things despite being many thousands of miles apart. Popular subjects are animals, patterns and shapes, and we find all of these at Altamira, including bison – now extinct in Europe. The outlines of the animals at Altamira were first either scratched into the rock or drawn in black charcoal. They were then painted in blacks, yellows and reds using natural colours called pigments.

Paintings of humans are relatively rare, although figures with both human and animal features were found in 2017 on the Indonesian island of Sulawesi. The figures in this hunting scene, which was created around 44,000 years ago, may not be humans at all but spirits. The mysterious figures show our ancestors had the imagination to think beyond the world they saw around them. We don't know why these paintings were created but archaeologists believe that they could be connected with storytelling, religion, rituals or communicating with spirits. In Europe they are often found further inside the caves than our ancestors were living and must have required great effort to create. We might never know the true meaning of these ancient artworks or why they were created but they show us that, for millennia, art has been an incredibly important part of being human.

HUMAN HANDS

Sulawesi is also home to some of the oldest paintings of a more popular subject – human hands. These date back around 40,000 years, but human hands have been found across the globe, and more recently people were painting them in Argentina, although that was still at least 9,500 years ago!

ROCK ART FROM AROUND THE WORLD

CHAUVET
France
Around 36,000 years old

ALTAMIRA
Spain
Around 35,000–15,000 years old

SERRA DA CAPIVARA
Brazil
At least 25,000 years ago

KAKADU
Australia
Over 20,000 years ago to the present

LASCAUX
France
Around 19,000 years old

CUEVA DE LAS MANOS
Argentina
13,000–9,500 years old

BHIMBETKA
India
Around 10,000 years ago to the present

MAGURA
Bulgaria
10,000–3,000 years ago

LAAS GEEL
Somaliland
3,500–2,500 years ago

RELIEF SCULPTURE

As well as painting in caves, our ancestors carved images into their walls. This is an early form of what we now refer to as relief sculpture. Relief sculpture is cut out of or into its background and is very often found on stone, but it can also be carved into materials such as wood, ivory and gems.

WE FIND RELIEFS all over the world, from enormous buildings to items as small as cups and rings. Some of the greatest ancient buildings are decorated with relief sculptures and these images played an important role. They were designed to send a message about the person or people who built them. They might record a great event or tell a story, which could be read a bit like a comic strip, or they might have important religious significance. These sculptures have many meanings and can give us evidence to show what the ancient world was like.

The tombs and temples of ancient Egypt were covered in vast amounts of reliefs which were often brightly painted. The sculptures give us an exciting insight into the world of the Egyptians. We find images of the gods they worshipped, who often have animal heads, and the pharaohs who ruled over them, believed to be gods on earth. In some tombs, scenes of farming and hunting offer us a glimpse of daily life.

Around 3,500 years ago, Hatshepsut, one of Egypt's few female pharaohs, built a magnificent temple for herself so that she could be worshipped after her death. The walls are covered with low relief sculpture designed to show her power and divinity, including scenes from an expedition which was one of the major achievements of her reign. This was a trip to a mysterious land called Punt, the "land of the gods", thought to have been in East Africa. Decorating the walls of the temple are ships at sea, exotic animals, and the treasures collected in Punt, including whole myrrh trees.

Around 200 years later, Pharaoh Rameses II, known as Rameses the Great, used sunken relief to show off his military might. After he waged war with one of Egypt's great enemies, the Hittites from modern-day Turkey and Syria, he had depictions of himself as a victorious military leader in a chariot carved into temple walls. But it was all about his image – he didn't actually win!

The power of relief sculpture can be seen throughout history and still surrounds us. If you look at the buildings around you, you might see it for yourself.

ANGKOR WAT

The temple of Angkor Wat, built in Cambodia in the twelfth century, is decorated with hundreds upon hundreds of metres of reliefs. In the scenes we find King Suryavarman II, who had the temple built, and battles between gods and demons from Hindu sagas.

THE PARTHENON

In Athens the ancient Greeks decorated their most famous temple, the Parthenon, with painted high relief sculpture. On each side of the building they carved a different mythological battle, designed to symbolize Athenian victory over their enemies. On one side of the Parthenon, men fight centaurs; on the other, they battle with female warriors called Amazons.

TYPES OF RELIEF SCULPTURE

SIDE PROFILE

SUNKEN RELIEFS

are created when images are cut into their background. These reliefs were used mainly by the Egyptians and were quick to make as the sculptor only had to carve into the surface rather than cutting the background away. The Egyptians often used hieroglyphics in the background of their reliefs to explain what was happening in the scene.

SIDE PROFILE

LOW RELIEF

is often called bas-relief and means that the images stand out from their background, but not very far. They are made by cutting away the material around the figures so that they are raised.

HIGH RELIEF

sculpture sticks out much further from its background and looks more three-dimensional. Sometimes parts of a high relief sculpture aren't attached to the background at all, which is why some ancient examples are missing arms or legs.

MOULDING IN CLAY

Clay played a vital role in the lives of our ancestors and is so important that it appears in the myths and religions of numerous cultures as the material humans are made from. It can be formed into infinite useful and beautiful shapes, and when heated to a high temperature, which is known as firing, it hardens in those forms to make ceramic.

SHERDS OF POTTERY discovered in Yuchanyan Cave in southern China date back 18,000 years, making them some of the earliest ever discovered. The sherds were from two cooking vessels and whilst pottery was an important invention for the storage and cooking of food, from very early on it has had other important roles. Across the globe, pottery has been essential in all parts of life, including religion and burial.

A wealth of painted pottery survives from ancient Greece and their functions and decoration give us an insight into some of the most important events in Greek culture. We can see examples of the sports the Greeks competed in on their pottery, ranging from discus throwing to chariot racing. Athletic competitions were an important part of Greek life and had enormous religious importance. Every four years, citizens from all over the ancient Greek world, which stretched from Spain to Turkey, came together to compete in the Olympic Games, the first of which took place in Greece in 776 BCE. At games in the city of Athens, victorious athletes were awarded amphorae of olive oil decorated with a painting of their sport and the goddess Athena dressed in armour.

Athena's brother the wine god Dionysus often appears on pottery used at a type of party called a symposium. A symposium was an important part of the life of Athenian men, who gathered together to drink and talk. You couldn't have a party without pottery, and different types were used to store and drink wine. On the pottery we find gods and heroes in scenes from mythology. We can usually spot gods by their accessories – often, Hermes the messenger god wears winged sandals and Artemis the huntress carries a bow and arrow. The artists who painted the pots might also label the figures depicted and write what they were saying as if it was coming out of their mouth, like an ancient speech bubble.

Some of the greatest advances in ceramic creation and decoration have taken place in China. One of the most important uses of clay was to make sculptures – sometimes on a vast scale, as with the Terracotta Army. Thousands of years after the army statues were buried, clay continues to be part of our daily lives and remains one of our most important materials.

TERRACOTTA ARMY

An 8,000 strong sculptural group was created 2,200 years ago for the enormous burial of the first emperor of China, Qin Shi Huang. 700,000 people worked to create what is the biggest ancient royal burial site in the world. The figures were made from terracotta, a red-brown clay, and the detail, down to the variety of hairstyles and facial features, makes each of the warriors feel like an individual. The once colourful warriors were armed with bronze weapons, terracotta chariots and horses, and were intended to guard the emperor in the afterlife.

GREEK POTTERY

Amphora – These pots were used for storing things like grain or wine. This one shows the Greek mythological heroes Ajax and Achilles playing dice.

Skythos – Men used these drinking cups at symposia. This one shows two athletes competing in pankration, a mixture of wrestling and boxing.

Hydria – These water jugs have three handles, two for carrying and one at the back for pouring. This example shows women filling theirs up at a water fountain.

Lekythos – These held oil. This one is a white-ground lekythos used in funeral rituals, depicting two people by a grave.

Epinetron – This unusual type of pottery was used by the Greeks to cover their thighs whilst they prepared wool for weaving.

Kylix – Large eyes like this are common on a kylix. When you lifted up the cup to drink, it would cover your face like a mask.

Krater – The Greeks used vessels like this to mix their wine with water. The artist Euphronios painted this one showing the body of the hero Sarpedon who died in the Trojan War.

Pyxis – These containers might hold jewellery or cosmetics. This one is decorated with a scene from the marriage of Achilles's parents, the goddess Thetis and a Greek king called Peleus.

Dinos – A mixing vessel for wine, this dinos on a stand shows the gods arriving at the wedding of Thetis and Peleus as well as mythological and real animals.

BRONZE SCULPTURES

Bronze transformed our lives and our art when it first came into use over 5,000 years ago. It was made by mixing copper and tin, which combine to make a strong and versatile metal alloy. Since its invention it has been used for vessels, weapons, mirrors, musical instruments and religious objects.

ALTHOUGH WHEN WE THINK of ancient Greek sculpture we often picture gleaming white marble, bronzes were actually some of the Greeks' most highly prized works of art. They are now rare, as most were either lost or plundered and melted down, but they were more popular than stone sculptures during the classical period of the fifth and fourth centuries BCE. Luckily, we do know what some of the greatest Greek bronzes looked like because they were copied in marble by the Romans. Two of the finest Greek bronze sculptures were rescued from the sea in 1972. A diver off the coast of Italy had spotted what he thought was the arm of a corpse but when he went to touch it, he realized it was made of bronze. What he had found were two life-sized sculptures of warriors. They are now known as the Riace bronzes, after the area where they were discovered. Both men would have been holding spears in one hand and propping up a shield in the other. One of the warriors has silver teeth and both have lips, nipples and eyelashes made from copper. We don't know exactly where the pair came from or where they were going, but their survival gives us a rare insight into the incredible ancient bronzes that have been lost.

Statues like this were made by lost wax casting, a technique found around the world, with very ancient examples in India and the Near East. In Nigeria the direct lost wax technique was used in casting bronze and other copper alloys to make a range of sculptures, from naturalistic heads to leopards. The incredibly lifelike Ife Head was cast from brass using the lost wax method in Nigeria in the fifteenth century. We don't know why the sculpture was created, but the head wears a crown and the face is covered in ridges which may be intended to show scarification, where the body is marked by designs through cutting or scratching.

Although the secrets of why some bronzes were made are still unknown, our love for bronze has lived on. Today many of the public sculptures in our towns and cities are made from this incredible alloy.

SANXINGDUI

In 1986 archaeologists at a site called Sanxingdui in China revealed hundreds of bronze artefacts dating back around 3,000 years. They had been made by a long-lost people and were burnt and broken before being buried in two pits along with elephant tusks, jade and gold in what is believed to have been a religious ritual. Amongst this incredible hoard were human sculptures which were several metres tall, a tree with fruit and bird ornaments hanging from its branches, large masks, and fifty-seven heads – some of which have been interpreted as belonging to witches and chiefs. These sculptures were not naturalistic like the Ife Head but have exaggerated features such as protruding eyes.

INDIRECT LOST WAX CASTING

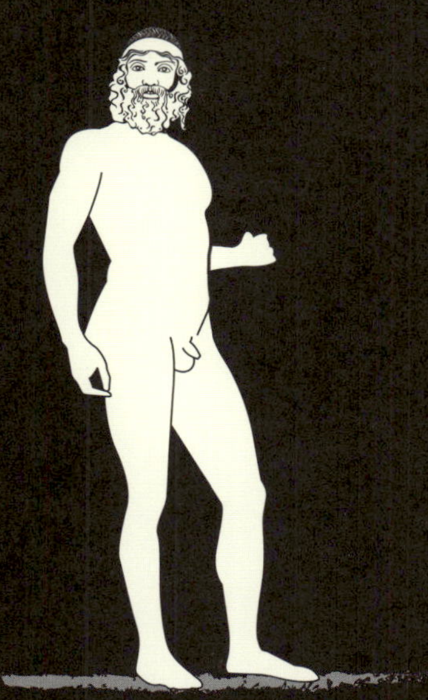

1. First a model is made for the sculpture, usually from clay.

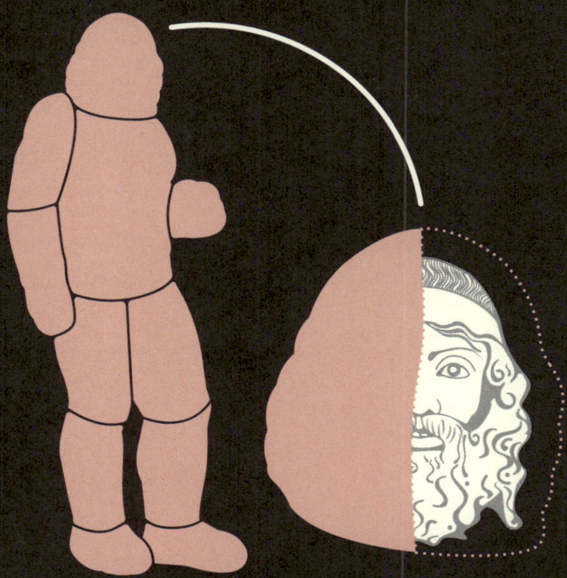

2. Moulds of clay or plaster are formed around the model in sections and dried.

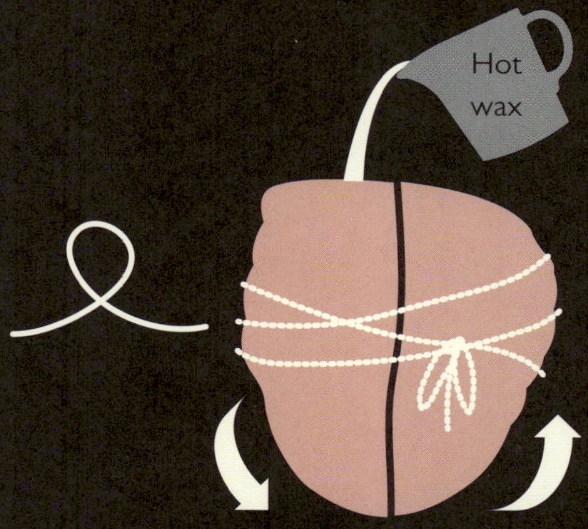

3. The mould pieces are reassembled and hot wax is poured inside in a thin layer to make a replica of the original model.

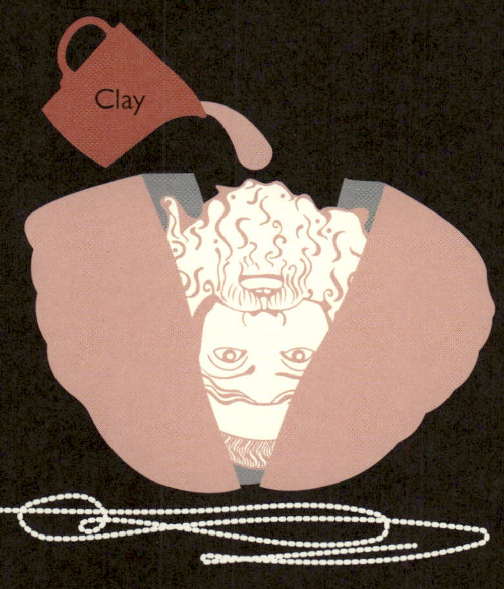

4. A clay mixture is poured inside the wax layer to make a core and the mould is removed revealing the wax image. The sculptor can change details at this point by adding more wax.

5. Metal pins are added to hold the core in place as well as a series of wax channels, funnels and vents to allow the bronze to be poured in and gases to escape.

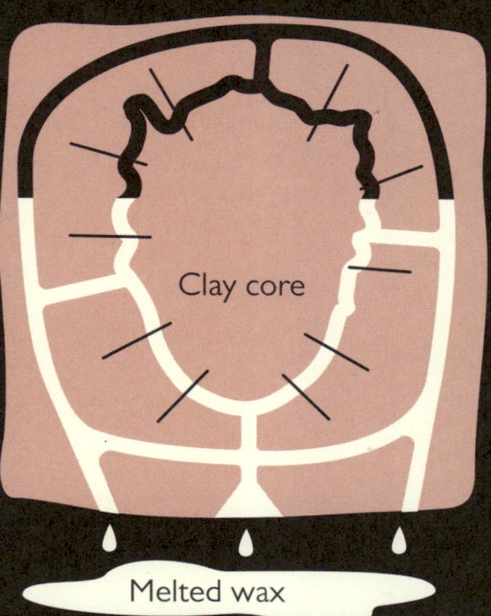

6. The model is then encased in clay and heated so the wax melts away leaving a mould.

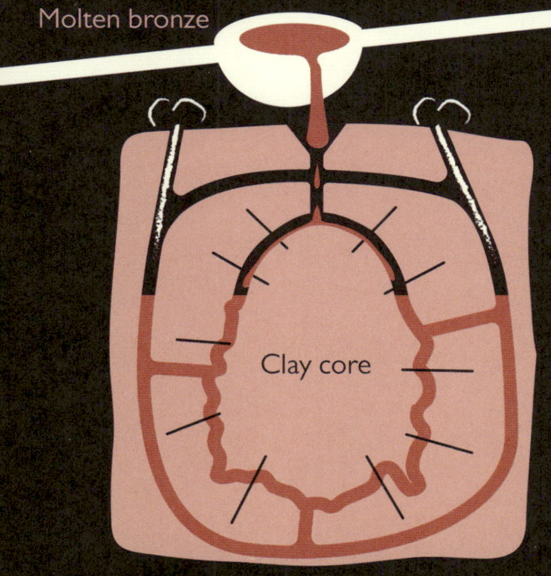

7. Molten bronze is poured into the mould and surrounds the clay core.

8. After the metal cools, the mould is broken open to reveal the section of the statue.

9. The channels and pins are removed and it can now be added to the rest of the sculpture using molten metal.

MOSAICS

Mosaics have been created for over 5,000 years. They come in a range of different forms, from intricate patterns to vast battle scenes, and are commonly made using pieces of stone, tile or glass.

MOSAICS ARE POPULAR all over the globe. Across the Islamic world, mosaics made using colourful tiles were used to decorate palaces and mosques in complex geometric patterns, and the Romans used mosaics to decorate the floors and walls of their homes with scenes ranging from historical battles to sea life. After the fall of the Roman Empire, mosaics continued to be popular into the Byzantine era which followed, and some of the greatest works of Byzantine art are the mosaics in the Italian city of Ravenna at the Basilica of San Vitale. Built in the sixth century, this church glistens with colourful mosaic decoration, much of it gold.

SAN VITALE

The mosaics of San Vitale depict religious scenes as well as the Emperor Justinian and his wife, Theodora, with golden halos and dressed in imperial purple to show their status.

Gold may have been one of the most prized materials in Europe, but across the Atlantic it was a different story. In 1519 Hernán Cortés, a Spanish conquistador, which means conqueror, set sail for Mexico with eleven ships, about six hundred men – and cannons. Cortés was on the hunt for gold and had heard rumours of a rich and powerful ruler. At that time, the land stretching from the Gulf of Mexico to the Pacific was inhabited by the Aztecs, whose ruler was called Moctezuma II. The Aztecs believed that Cortés was a god and sent him treasures including items of gold along with something far more valuable to them – turquoise.

The blue-green mineral turquoise held great religious importance to the Aztecs, and mosaics created using the precious stone are thought to have been used in their rituals. In fact, cultures throughout Central America valued turquoise, and the Mixtec peoples, who had incredible mosaic expertise, may have been the original makers of the Aztecs' treasures. Xiuhtecuhtli, the fire god whose name means "Turquoise Lord", was often pictured wearing the precious stone and some turquoise mosaic masks, thought to represent gods, may have been worn to act out stories. A turquoise mosaic serpent with two heads, mother of pearl for its teeth and red shells around its mouth and nostrils might have been worn by a priest during a ritual. Snakes were thought to be powerful creatures, and a feathered serpent was the symbol of the god Quetzalcoatl, whom the Aztecs believed Cortés to be.

AZTEC FEATHERWORK

The Aztecs also used feathers from a range of birds, including parrots and hummingbirds, to make mosaics. The most prestigious feathers were green from the quetzal bird but we also see reds, yellows and blues.

Since Cortés first landed in Mexico, Aztec gold has been melted down into bars, turquoise mosaics have become rare museum items and much featherwork has been lost. We are very lucky that some of the Aztecs' most exquisite artworks survived the conquistadors.

MOSAIC FACES

Left
This mask dates to between 1400 and 1521. It was made from wood and covered with turquoise mosaic pieces. It once had golden eyelids and its teeth are made from conch shell. It might be the Aztec god, Xiuhtecuhtli, or the lumps on the mask might show the warts of the sun god, Tonatiuh.

Right
This section of mosaic from the Basilica of San Vitale in Ravenna depicts Empress Theodora, a former actress. It was made using coloured glass, and the golden pieces which make up her jewellery were created by adding real gold to the glass.

GOTHIC ART

In the twelfth century a new style of art and architecture was born in Europe. Known as Gothic, it transformed Christian art, and the masterpieces of this period are soaring and sparkling stained glass windows.

SOME OF THE MOST JAW-DROPPING examples of Gothic art can be found in places of worship. This was because the Gothic style transformed how cathedrals and churches were built. Before this, cathedrals were dark and gloomy places, with the heavy weight of their arched roofs, known as ceiling vaults, carried by thick walls which could only contain small windows. Gothic architects developed ways for the vaulted ceilings to be lighter and for the weight to be carried with extra supports. This led to the construction of buildings which soared to the heavens and towered over cities across Europe.

Two key inventions made these dizzyingly high ceilings and thin walls possible. Ribbed vaults are a series of connected pointed arches, the "ribs", which provide more support for the ceilings. And flying buttresses on the outside of the buildings are like arms carrying the pressure of the roof away from the walls. The largest Gothic cathedral in France is in the city of Amiens, where the ceilings are over forty-two metres high.

THE SAINTE-CHAPELLE

The Gothic chapel of Sainte-Chapelle in Paris is small by the standards of Amiens but still would have been a dominant feature on the city's skyline when it was built in the thirteenth century. It took just seven years to complete and was intended to house religious relics which King Louis IX brought to France, including the Crown of Thorns worn by Jesus Christ at his crucifixion.

People who came to worship in these Gothic cathedrals and churches might encounter sculptures carved in ivory or beautiful gold work, but by far the most awe-inspiring sight would be something else. The thinner walls and sky-high roofs had made way for some of the most spectacular Christian paintings in medieval Europe – stained-glass windows. These enormous, colourful windows depicted religious scenes and allowed brilliant light, which was thought to be holy, into the vast spaces. The windows were created by first drawing out the window design and then cutting the different colours of glass into shapes which fitted together like a mosaic to form the drawn image. Details, such as the way someone's clothing is draped, the curls of their hair and their facial features, were then painted on to the coloured glass pieces. The glass would be fired to fuse this paint into the panes and once this was done, the window was fixed together using lead to bind the pieces in place.

The stained glass windows in the Sainte-Chapelle, the chapel built for Louis IX of France who later became a saint, depict the life of Christ and the discovery of the relics housed in the chapel. The building and its decoration were designed to show its visitors that kingship was sacred and that Paris was a holy city. Gothic stained-glass windows had the power to make their viewers feel as if they had been transported to heaven.

LIGHT IN THE SAINTE-CHAPELLE

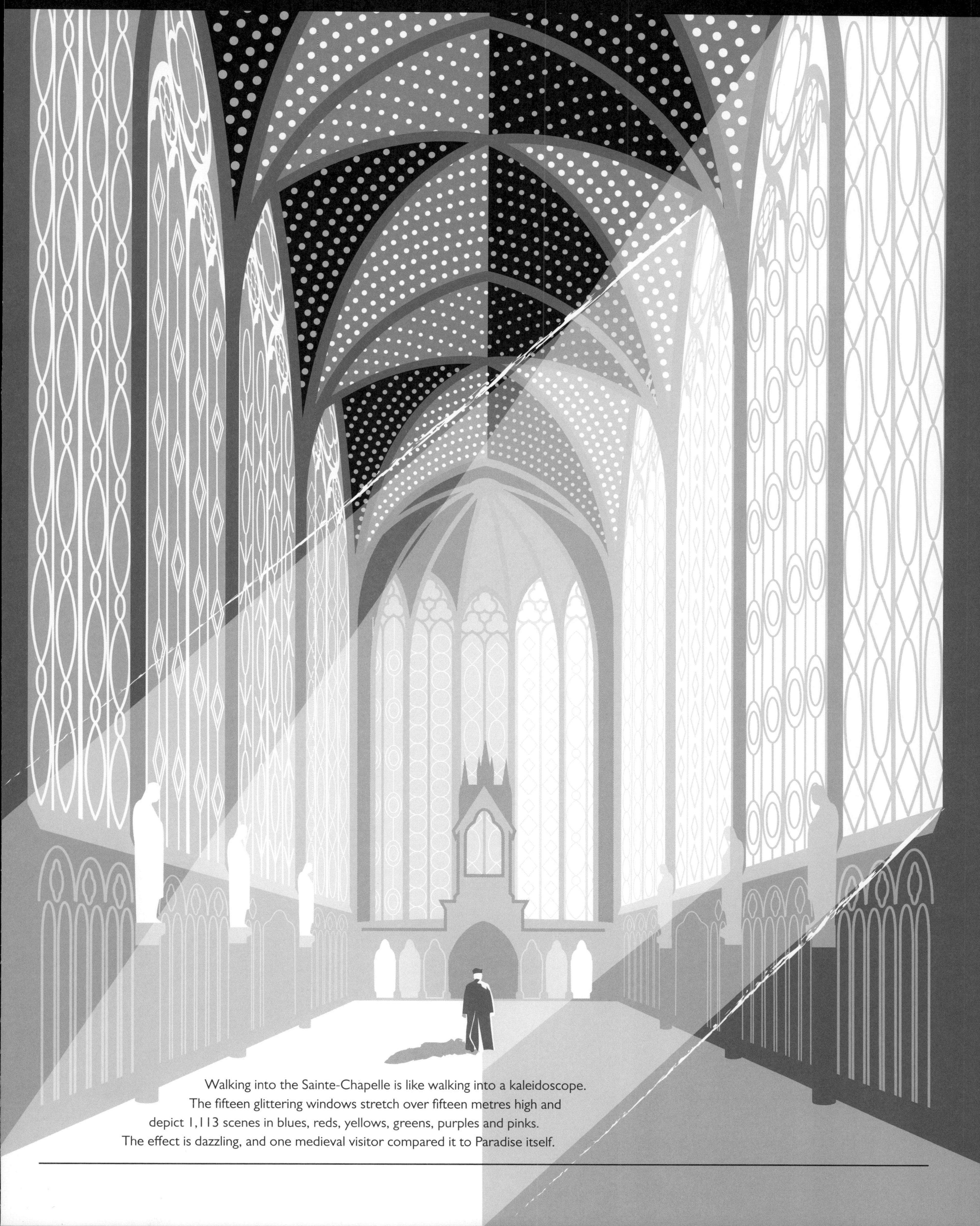

Walking into the Sainte-Chapelle is like walking into a kaleidoscope. The fifteen glittering windows stretch over fifteen metres high and depict 1,113 scenes in blues, reds, yellows, greens, purples and pinks. The effect is dazzling, and one medieval visitor compared it to Paradise itself.

RENAISSANCE ART

The fourteenth century saw the dawn of a new era in Europe but its origins were very much in the past. The era is called the Renaissance, which means "rebirth". Ancient Greek and Roman art and culture were rediscovered and given a new life.

RENAISSANCE ARTISTS took inspiration from a range of classical sources and some travelled to Rome to study the ancient art and ruins there. Art began to appear more realistic as artists looked closer at nature and the human body and discovered new techniques, such as perspective. Some of the greatest artists in history lived during this period and we are so familiar with them that we know them by single names – Michelangelo, Raphael, Donatello, Botticelli. But the Renaissance was not just about art. We can talk about Renaissance science, politics, literature and even gardens. One artist in particular can be described as a "Renaissance man" – Leonardo da Vinci.

Da Vinci designed weapons and flying machines, studied the flight of birds and drew incredibly accurate maps.

Da Vinci was born in Italy in 1452 and during his own lifetime he was extremely famous. When we hear his name, we immediately think of his paintings, and he is celebrated for depicting one of the most famous smiles in history – the "Mona Lisa". "The Last Supper", his mural in the dining room of a convent in Milan, is arguably his masterpiece. The scene, stretching 8.8 metres wide and 4.6 metres high, was painted from around 1495 to 1498 and shows Jesus Christ at his final dinner with his disciples. The viewer's gaze is drawn to Christ in the centre of the image due to da Vinci's masterly grasp of perspective, with each naturalistic figure surrounding him adding to the story with their gestures.

It's in looking at his drawings that we can see da Vinci was much more than an artist. They are often studies and illustrations of research which helped him reach the incredible heights he achieved in his paintings. He wanted his subjects to look as natural as possible, and to do so he went under the skin. During his life he dissected over thirty corpses to learn more about how the human body worked, and his detailed anatomical drawings demonstrate a profound knowledge of biology. If da Vinci's discoveries had been published, they would have changed the study of anatomy.

"MONA LISA"
Da Vinci began this painting in around 1503 and, although it was never finished, the Mona Lisa's innovative pose changed the way artists painted portraits.

Da Vinci wasn't just drawing to improve his art – art and science come together in his work. The drawings in his notebooks, annotated in mirror writing from right to left, demonstrate the wide range of areas in science, engineering and architecture which he explored. He was something of a perfectionist but his studies paid off. We might not have a large number of his paintings but what we do have is an insight into the mind of a genius.

"VITRUVIAN MAN"

"Vitruvian Man" is one of da Vinci's most famous drawings. It was created in pen and ink around 1490 and, appropriately for the Renaissance, its inspiration was ancient. The drawing is also known as "The Proportions of the Human Body According to Vitruvius" and the Vitruvius it refers to was a Roman engineer and architect who wrote ten books about architecture between 33 and 23 BCE. The books cover how to build everything from theatres to houses, and there are even sections on sundials and catapults.

In the Renaissance, when artists and architects grew fascinated by the ancient world, Vitruvius's writings became extremely influential. One of Vitruvius's ideas that preoccupied artists was to do with human proportion – that is, how the different parts of the body relate to one other and the whole body in size. What does that have to do with architecture? Well, Vitruvius thought that the proportions of temples should be based on the proportions of humans.

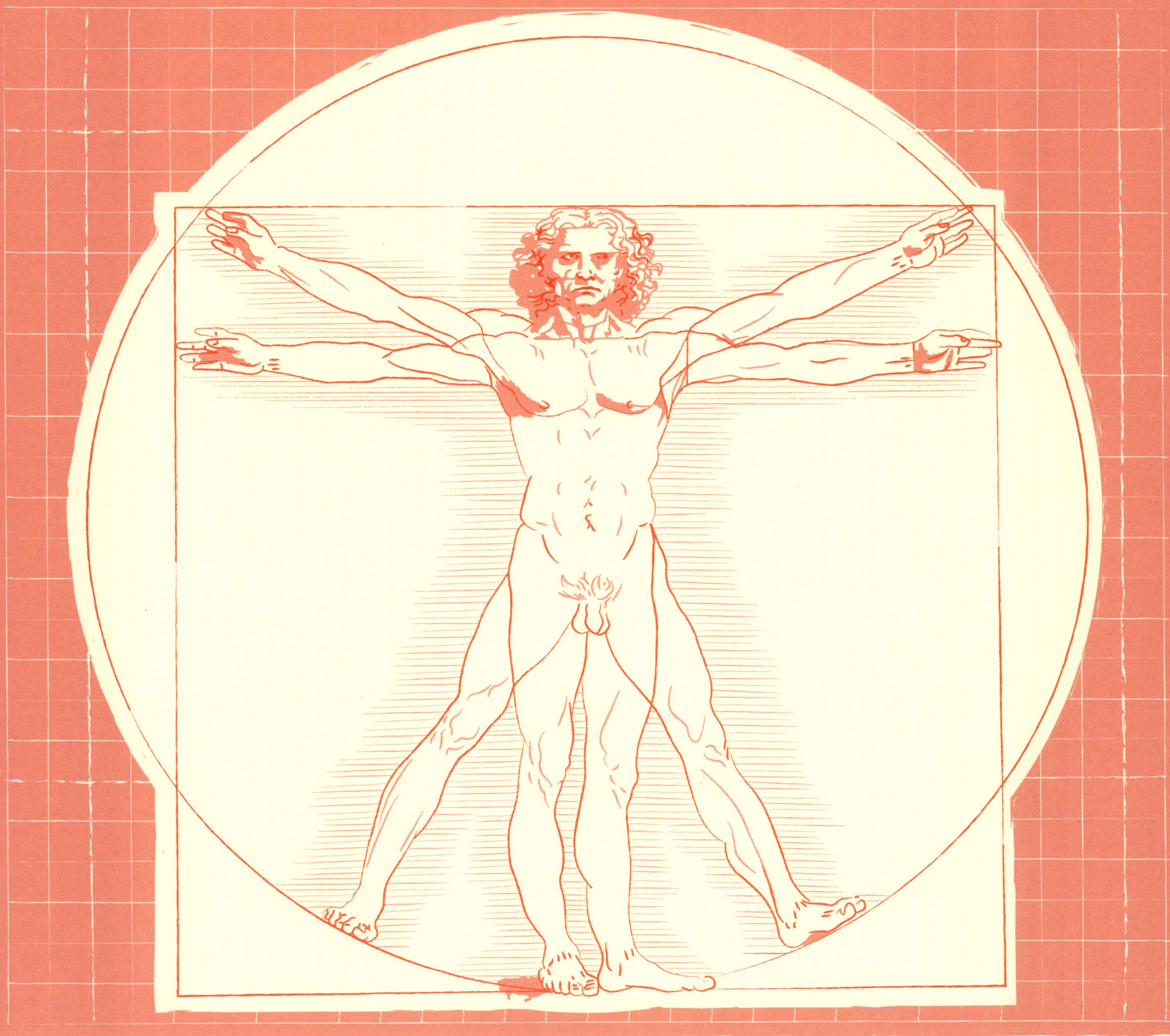

According to Vitruvius, a body is ten times the distance between the chin and the top of the forehead. That was the same distance, he wrote, as between the wrist and the tip of the middle finger. Vitruvius went on to describe the human body as fitting inside a square and a circle, and artists puzzled over how that might work as there were no surviving illustrations. There are actually other Vitruvian men by other artists attempting to sketch the description. Da Vinci's drawing takes inspiration from Vitruvius as well as his own observations of bodies and is surrounded by his notes written in mirror writing. For da Vinci, the body was a model for the world.

RELIGIOUS ART

Religion has had an enormous impact on the history of art since our earliest artistic creations. From illustrating religious texts to decorating places of worship to spreading ideas, art has been tied to religion in a whole host of ways.

IN 1939, A 40,000-YEAR-OLD figure with the head of a lion and a human's body was discovered in Germany. The 31-centimetre figure would have taken about 400 hours to carve from a mammoth tusk, an enormous task which shows its importance. We think the "Lion Man" is connected with the supernatural, and wear on its body may have come from being passed around in a community ritual. This would make it one of the earliest examples of religious art.

Art can play a part in worship and ritual; images might help people pray to their gods, for example. Pictures might tell a story to teach a lesson or strengthen people's faith. The making of a religious artwork can be a sacred process. We find art in many religions, from the relief sculpture of Hindu temples to colossal statues of the Buddha. Many mosques are decorated with ornate calligraphy of Islamic texts and elaborate patterns, and at the site of Dura-Europos in Syria is a synagogue from the third century CE decorated with biblical scenes and figures, a rare example in ancient Jewish art. By this period, Christian art was appearing in Roman tombs, and as the religion became more widespread in Europe, its impact on art increased. It was used for a range of purposes, including decoration, education and inspiration.

Religious art can inspire, it can decorate and it can bring people together.

The production of art in northern Europe flourished in the fifteenth and sixteenth centuries in a period that is known as the Northern Renaissance, and a huge amount of art from this time had a Christian purpose. This included many altarpieces.

The world's most famous altarpiece is found in the city of Ghent in Belgium, giving it its name – the Ghent Altarpiece. It was completed in 1432 and commissioned by a wealthy merchant called Jodocus Vijd for his private chapel in the Church of St John the Baptist, which has since become the Cathedral of St Bavo. The altarpiece was painted by two brothers, Hubert and Jan van Eyck, and is made up of twelve wooden panels with two wings; when these are open, the artwork stretches nearly five metres wide. The incredibly detailed and brilliantly colourful paintings are an example of the van Eycks' early mastery of oil painting. The Ghent Altarpiece has been saved from fire and rioters, and looted a number of times, including by the Nazis. It has become one of the most important artworks in the world and is just one example of the impact religion has had on art.

ALTARPIECES

Some of the most famous Northern Renaissance paintings are altarpieces – paintings of religious scenes positioned above, on or behind an altar. Some altarpieces are made of multiple wooden panels on hinges so they can be opened and closed to reveal different paintings. This is usually done on special days, such as feasts.

THE GHENT ALTARPIECE

When the altarpiece is closed, we see twelve scenes, including the angel Gabriel visiting the Virgin Mary to tell her that she will be the mother of Jesus Christ. Below, St John the Baptist and St John the Evangelist are painted in grey to look like stone sculptures and there are portraits of Jodocus Vijd and his wife, Elisabeth Borluut, praying on either side.

Opened up, fourteen further paintings are revealed. On the wings, we find Adam and Eve as well as choirs of angels, and at the top in the central panel God the Father sits on a throne. Mary and John the Baptist are at either side, and below is the scene known as *The Adoration of the Mystic Lamb*. Here a crowd of saints are gathered around a lamb being sacrificed upon an altar, its blood pouring into a golden cup, symbolizing the sacrifice of Jesus when he died on the cross.

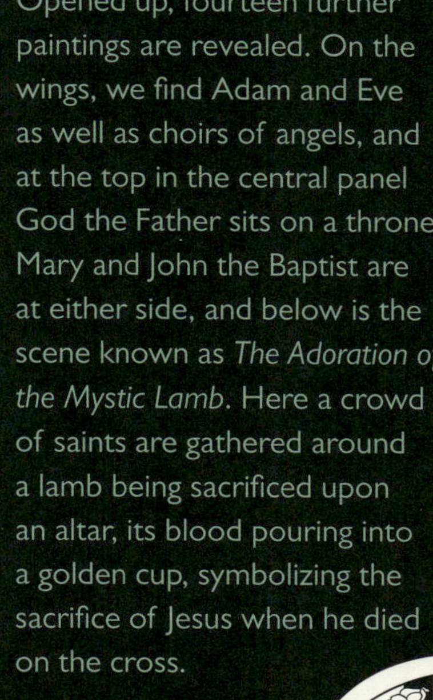

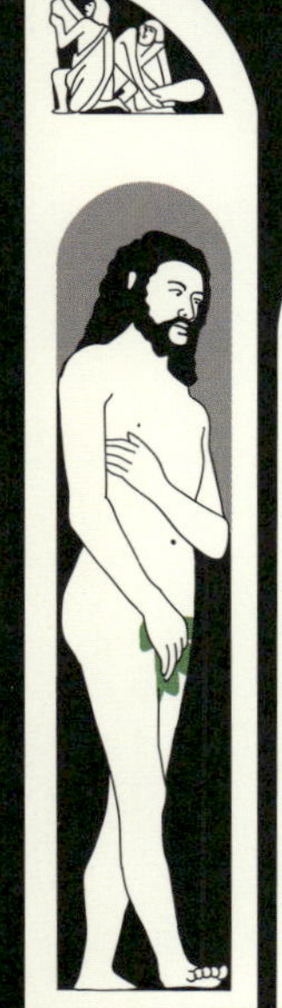

FRESCOES

For thousands of years, some of our greatest artworks have been painted on walls and ceilings. These artworks are captured in the plaster of the surface and are called frescoes, meaning "fresh" in Italian.

THE MINOANS, who lived on the island of Crete from around 3000 to 1000 BCE, produced some of the earliest surviving frescoes. Other ancient cultures created their frescoes by painting onto dry plaster – the material which coated their walls – but the Minoans were one of the earliest to start painting on to wet plaster. This method, known as *buon fresco* ("true" fresco), means that the paintings are fixed in place as the plaster dries. Several thousand years later in the early fourteenth century, an Italian artist called Giotto created a series of frescoes which marked a turning point in art history. He painted scenes from the lives of the Virgin Mary and Jesus Christ on the walls of a chapel in Padua, Italy, which broke away from the flat images of the Byzantine era. Looking at these frescoes feels as though we are looking at living people in three-dimensional places.

A striking fresco of a young man leaping over a bull shows us what we think was a rite of passage in Minoan society.

Giotto's frescoes paved the way for Renaissance painters to take this technique to new heights with their knowledge of anatomy and perspective. But it was a reluctant artist who would create the world's most famous example. In 1508 Michelangelo began work on decorating the ceiling of the Sistine Chapel in Rome with an elaborate fresco. This was an incredibly important job – it is the pope's own chapel – and initially Michelangelo had declined, since he saw himself as more of a sculptor than a painter. Thankfully for us, he finally agreed.

The ceiling is well over five hundred square metres but Michelangelo completed it in just four years, which included breaks. Some accounts say that he had no assistants but even if he did, which is likely, they all must have worked at lightning speed. The ceiling depicts nine scenes in glorious colours which break into three groups – God's creation of the world, the story of Adam and Eve and their banishment from the Garden of Eden, and Noah and the Flood. But Michelangelo did not limit himself to these nine scenes. The ceiling around them is alive with upwards of three hundred figures who seem so real that they look like they might fall down on you. Some people think he even painted himself into the fresco as a prophet called Jeremiah.

Every year millions of tourists visit the Sistine Chapel and strain their necks to see Michelangelo's masterpiece. He proved himself wrong – he really could paint.

THE SISTINE CHAPEL

The Sistine Chapel ceiling is around twenty metres high, so how was Michelangelo able to reach it? Well, luckily, he was one of the great Renaissance all-rounders, and he used his engineering skill to design special scaffolding which arched like a bridge under the ceiling. And he didn't stop there – he was also a poet, and wrote a sonnet for a friend in which he described how he bent his body back to reach the ceiling with his brush, which dripped paint onto his face as he worked. He sketched a self-portrait of himself in this uncomfortable position beside the poem.

THE SISTINE CHAPEL CEILING

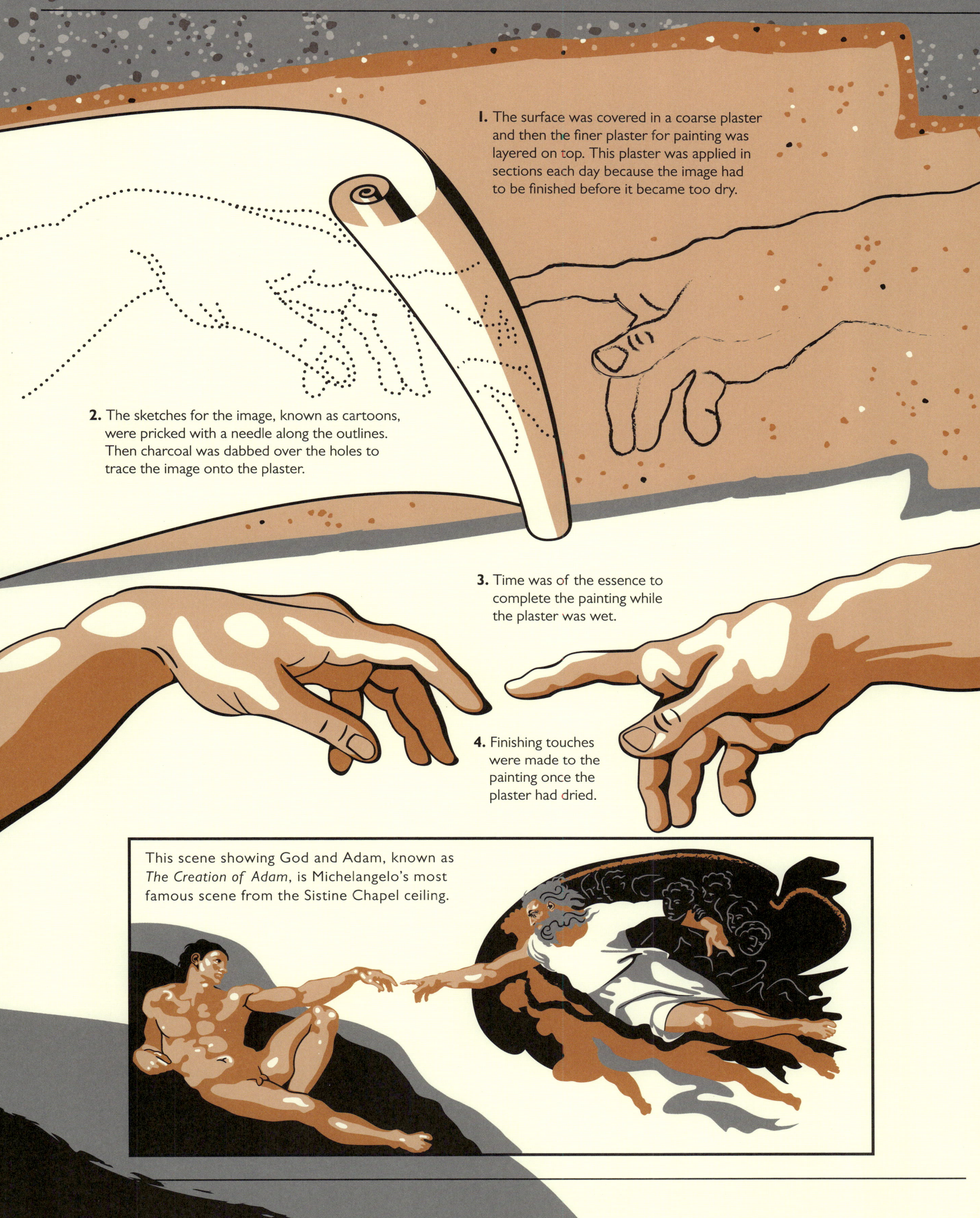

This scene showing God and Adam, known as *The Creation of Adam*, is Michelangelo's most famous scene from the Sistine Chapel ceiling.

PERSPECTIVE

Perspective is used to create the illusion of three dimensions on two-dimensional surfaces. Artists use different types of perspective to try to reproduce how our eyes see the world around us.

DURING THE RENAISSANCE in Europe, perspective became one of the important tools artists used to create natural-looking scenes. The invention of linear perspective is credited to the Italian sculptor and architect Filippo Brunelleschi in the early fifteenth century. Many different artists, including Donatello, Raphael and Leonardo da Vinci, experimented with perspective and used it to create artworks which capture a strikingly realistic sense of space and depth, despite being made on flat surfaces such as canvases and walls.

The use of linear perspective spread but before it reached artists in northern Europe they used a different method to create the illusion of space. They mastered using colour to mimic the effects of the atmosphere to make things appear further away. Distant mountains were painted bluer and lighter and skies grow paler as they come closer to the horizon, as if they are being diluted. Leonardo Da Vinci used this method in his paintings and he gave it its name – aerial perspective.

Painters also used a device called foreshortening to create depth. In the late fifteenth century, Italian artist Andrea Mantegna created one of the most famous examples of this technique. In his painting "Lamentation over the Dead Christ", Christ lies on his back on a slab with his feet facing us, complete with holes from the crucifixion nails. His body looks as if it stretches away from us because Mantegna has shortened it in the painting.

Foreshortening and linear perspective are vital components in *trompe l'oeil* painting, which means "deceive the eye" in French. The seventeenth-century painter Andrea Pozzo was a master of *trompe l'oeil*. His decoration of the flat ceiling of the church of Sant'Ignazio in Rome creates the feeling that the building reaches up even higher than it really does, opening out to the heavens.

From the nineteenth century, some artists moved away from perspective and experimented with other ways of painting, but its clever use has certainly continued. Bridget Riley uses perspective in her paintings to make them look like they're moving. She paints dots and lines which seem to fold in on themselves, ripple like waves or spiral away from us. Despite being a centuries-old invention, perspective remains a tool which truly brings art to life.

LINEAR PERSPECTIVE

This is created by adding a point on the horizon, known as a vanishing point, which is where parallel lines meet, in the same way that if we looked down a railway track it would seem to disappear on the horizon. Objects which are supposed to be closer to our eye will be further away from the vanishing point and look bigger. When objects are closer to the vanishing point, they will be smaller and therefore look further away.

BRUNELLESCHI'S EXPERIMENT

Painting with polished silver sky

Mirror

In the early 1400s Brunelleschi demonstrated his invention of perspective. He created a painting on a panel of the baptistry building in Florence and covered the sky with polished silver to reflect the real sky. In the middle of the painting was a hole as small as a lentil where the vanishing point would be.

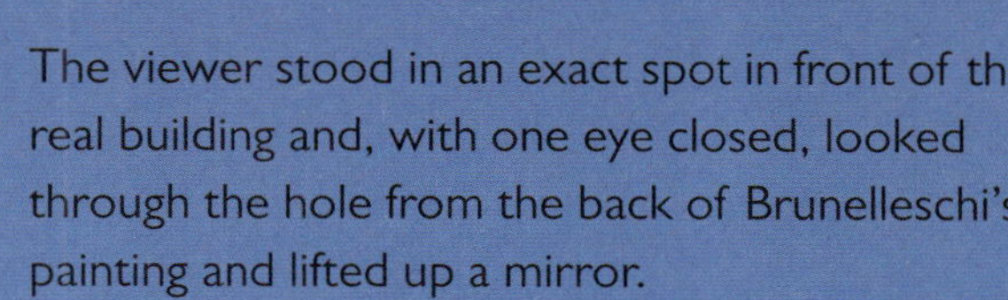

The viewer stood in an exact spot in front of the real building and, with one eye closed, looked through the hole from the back of Brunelleschi's painting and lifted up a mirror.

By holding the mirror in front of them to reflect the painting and then lowering it, the viewer could see that looking at Brunelleschi's painting was exactly like looking at the real building from that position.

THE PAINTED PAGE

For centuries cultures around the world have decorated pages for books, manuscripts and albums. These vibrant and richly detailed painted pages have gone on to inspire new types and styles of art.

FOR OVER A THOUSAND YEARS Christian texts were lit up, or "illuminated", with ornate letters and scenes in gold and bright colours. One of the finest examples is *The Book of Kells*, thought to have been created on the Scottish island of Iona around 800 CE. This Latin manuscript contains the four Gospels which tell the story of the life of Jesus Christ. It was created on animal skin and its hundreds of pages are adorned with portraits of saints, images of beasts and letters embellished with elaborate knot designs. Paintings in manuscripts are called miniatures – which isn't because they are small, although they often are – but from *minium*, the Latin word for the red paint used for special letters. It is from these illuminated manuscripts and their miniatures that the tradition of the miniature portrait evolved.

Early examples of illuminated texts were made by monks and religious figures to be displayed or to be carried around by individuals.

In Islamic art, books have been made beautiful through gold gilding, elaborate patterns, painted illustrations and complex artistic writing called calligraphy. In 1526 a dynasty was established which developed a distinctive style from these traditions – the Mughals. Its founder was a Muslim prince named Babur, who took control of a small kingdom in Afghanistan and conquered into northern India. His son Humayun set the course for the development of the Mughal style. Forced into exile by his enemies, he sought safety in Persia (modern-day Iran) at the royal court, which had a tradition of painting manuscripts. When Humayun returned to his empire, two artists came with him – Mir Sayyid Ali and 'Abd al-Samad. They had an enormous influence on Mughal painting, which combined the Persian style with that of Indian artists. Art brought to the Mughal court by European envoys, travellers and traders also influenced the style's depiction of light and depth.

Akbar, the next emperor, had workshops made up of artists, calligraphers, and craftspeople who worked together to create illuminated manuscripts. He commissioned the *Hamzanama*, or *Tales of Hamza*. This tells the story of Amir Hamza, the uncle of the Prophet Muhammad, and his adventures in his quest to spread Islam. It took over one hundred artists and craftspeople to create.

Akbar's son Jahangir preferred portraits and paintings of nature to illustrated texts. During his reign, an artist called Ustad Mansur created some of the most delicate paintings of wildlife. He was given the title "Wonder of the Age" and it is through work like his that we can see the artistry of the painted page.

THE *HAMZANAMA*

This took fifteen years to complete, and 1,400 paintings were created on cotton for the project. As well as Hamza, we find people with elephant ears, giants, witches and demons. The exquisitely detailed paintings bursting with vibrant colour are amongst some of the greatest works of Islamic painting.

This bird, called a Himalayan blue-throated barbet, was created by Mansur around 1610–25 and is the type of painting which could have been bound in an album.

SCULPTURE

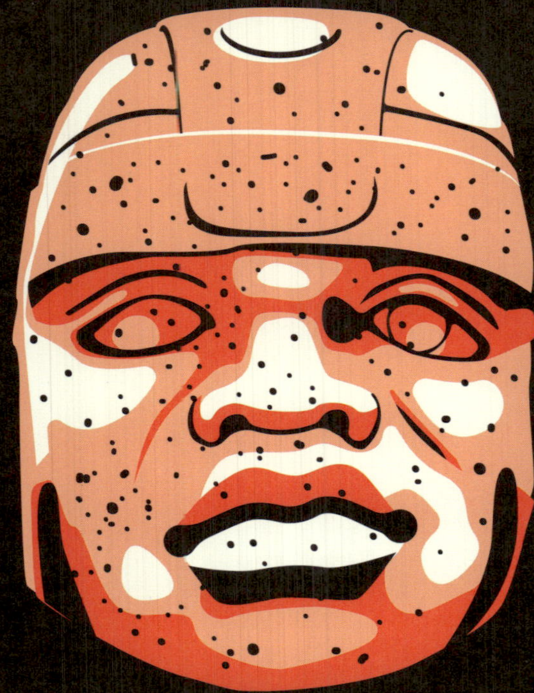

OLMEC HEAD

The Olmec civilization flourished between 1400 and 400 BCE around the Gulf of Mexico and was the oldest culture to create large scale art in that part of the world. They are famous for 17 colossal stone heads, some almost 3 metres tall, which were carved from massively heavy stones hauled with great effort over large distances. Each of the heads looks like an individual, and they are thought to be portraits of rulers, designed to show their power.

NEO-ASSYRIAN LAMASSU

The Neo-Assyrians ruled from 972–612 BCE and created the largest empire the world had seen, covering Iraq, Syria and Lebanon and reaching into Egypt, Iran and Turkey. King Ashurnasirpal II built a great palace in modern-day Iraq at a site called Nimrud. This winged lion with the head of a man is called a lamassu and is part of a pair carved from stone which were thought to give magical protection. It has five legs so that from the front it appears to be standing still but from the side it looks to be striding forward.

LESHAN GIANT BUDDHA

At 71 metres high, this sculpture carved from a cliff face in China is the largest stone statue of the Buddha in the world. Work was begun by a monk called Haitong in 713 CE and it took ninety years to complete. Three rivers meet at the statue's feet and the story goes that Haitong created the sculpture to calm the water and protect sailors. It was covered with a clay mixture, and the facial features, hands, feet and the folds in the robes were painted.

THE STAR HOUSE POLE

This totem pole comes from the Haida Nation, a people who live on small islands off the western coast of Canada. It was raised outside the Star House in the village of Old Massett in 1879 by Chief Anetlas after he and his wife adopted their daughter. After the 11.36-metre wooden pole was carved, black, red and blue-green paint was used to highlight details. At the bottom of the pole is a raven which may represent a crest. Further up the pole is a grizzly bear with a human captive which might refer to the tale of a girl kidnapped by bears.

For thousands of years, people around the world have carved stone and wood into enormous sculptures. They are created for many different purposes and carry many different meanings.

MOAI

Easter Island, known as Rapa Nui to its inhabitants, is one of the most remote places in the world where humans have settled. Between 1100 and 1650 the Rapa Nui created around 900 stone sculptures called moai, with an average height of 20 metres. They depict ancestral chiefs descended from gods and were believed to have supernatural powers. They were usually positioned near the coast facing inwards to watch over the island, and would have needed groups of around 40 people to move them into place.

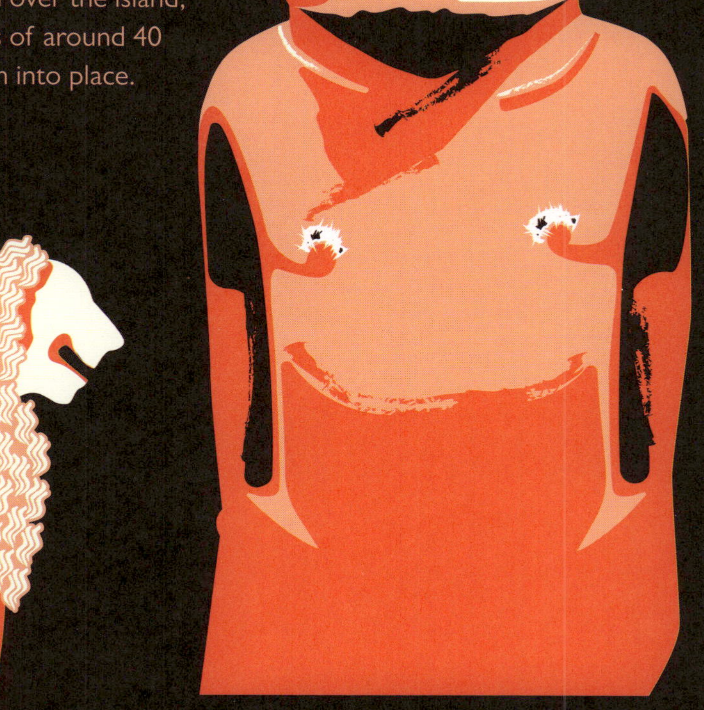

TEMPLE FIGURE OF KU-KA'ILI-MOKU

This wooden temple sculpture, called a ki'i, depicts the Hawaiian war god, Ku-ka'ili-moku – Ku the island snatcher – and stands over 2.5 metres tall. Carved between 1790 and 1819, it may have been intended to act as a way for the god to enter the temple. Its bent arms and knees suggests it's ready for action, and its chin juts forward, mouth open in an expression of disrespect. The long hair is formed of rows of pig or dog heads.

LION CAPITAL OF A PILLAR OF ASHOKA

In 268 BCE Ashoka inherited the Mauryan empire which covered most of India. He expanded his lands even further but felt such remorse for the slaughter he caused that he turned to Buddhism. He promoted his new way of life to his subjects by inscribing messages on 12-metre-high pillars across his Empire, which were topped with some of India's earliest stone sculptures. At the top of his most famous pillar, resting on an upside-down lotus flower, are four roaring lions who stand on a wheel depicting a horse, a bull, a lion and an elephant in relief.

THE GREAT SPHINX OF GIZA

This is one of the world's most famous sculptures and lies beside the Pyramids at Giza in Egypt. It's gigantic at approximately 20 metres high and 73 metres long and was carved over four and a half thousand years ago around 2500 BCE. A sphinx is a mythical animal, usually with a human head and the body of a lion, and this one wears a royal headdress. Some think that it was carved to resemble the pharaoh at the time, Khafre. The Sphinx was buried beneath the sands with only its head emerging until 1817.

THE BODY

In art there are human figures everywhere, and they all look very different. One of the oldest artworks in the world is a six-centimetre figure of a woman dating back around 40,000 years. She isn't exactly realistic, but she probably wasn't supposed to be. Our desire to depict bodies in all manner of different ways has continued ever since.

THE CARVINGS OF PHARAOHS on Egyptian temples look totally different from the enormous stone figures that stand on Easter Island, which in turn look nothing like the paintings of people who fill Mughal albums. Bodies are depicted differently in different cultures.

For over two thousand years in Europe, many artists made it their mission to depict lifelike bodies. But although these bodies look real, they are often not realistic. Artists wanted to portray what they thought was a "perfect" body so they idealized their subjects. The ancient Greek sculptor Polykleitos was one of the most famous artists in the ancient world. He wanted to depict an ideal male body, and his statue "Doryphoros" ("spear carrier" in Greek) is his masterpiece. His pose creates the feeling of lifelike movement and is known as *contrapposto*, which became one of the most important poses in Western art.

USING OUR BODIES IN ART

We don't just try to recreate bodies in our art – our bodies become part of it. Our ancestors used their hands as stencils on cave walls, performance artists use their own bodies in their work, and cultures in Micronesia and Polynesia have a history of tattooing their bodies in decorative designs connected with religion and identity.

Contrapposto** **is a pose in which the weight rests on one leg, creating a curve.

Portraying bodies realistically was not important in medieval art and they often look flat. But in the Renaissance, artists once again made it their mission to depict bodies which looked natural and three-dimensional. They often carried out dissections on dead bodies to understand how the body worked and bring their artworks to life. And art helped science, too. Andreas Vesalius was a groundbreaking anatomist in the sixteenth century whose incredibly influential book *On the Fabric of the Human Body* was illustrated by artists.

After the Renaissance, the Grand Manner style took hold. In this style, artists copied the poses of classical statues in their painting and aimed for bodies to look perfect and ideal. Art students continued to study anatomy, drew from copies of classical sculptures and attended life drawing classes to sketch naked models – although women were banned from these lessons because it wasn't thought proper for them to take part. But in the late nineteenth century, artists began thinking beyond classical inspirations and by the twentieth century, artists were seeking inspiration from Africa and ancient Egypt, breaking the rules of perspective and depicting bodies from their imagination. The Swiss artist Alberto Giacometti stretched bodies in his sculptures, making them look almost like skeletons, and the French artist Henri Matisse painted them in unnaturally bright colours. The body continues to be one of art's favourite subjects and one thing is for sure – we still love looking at ourselves.

SCULPTING THE BODY

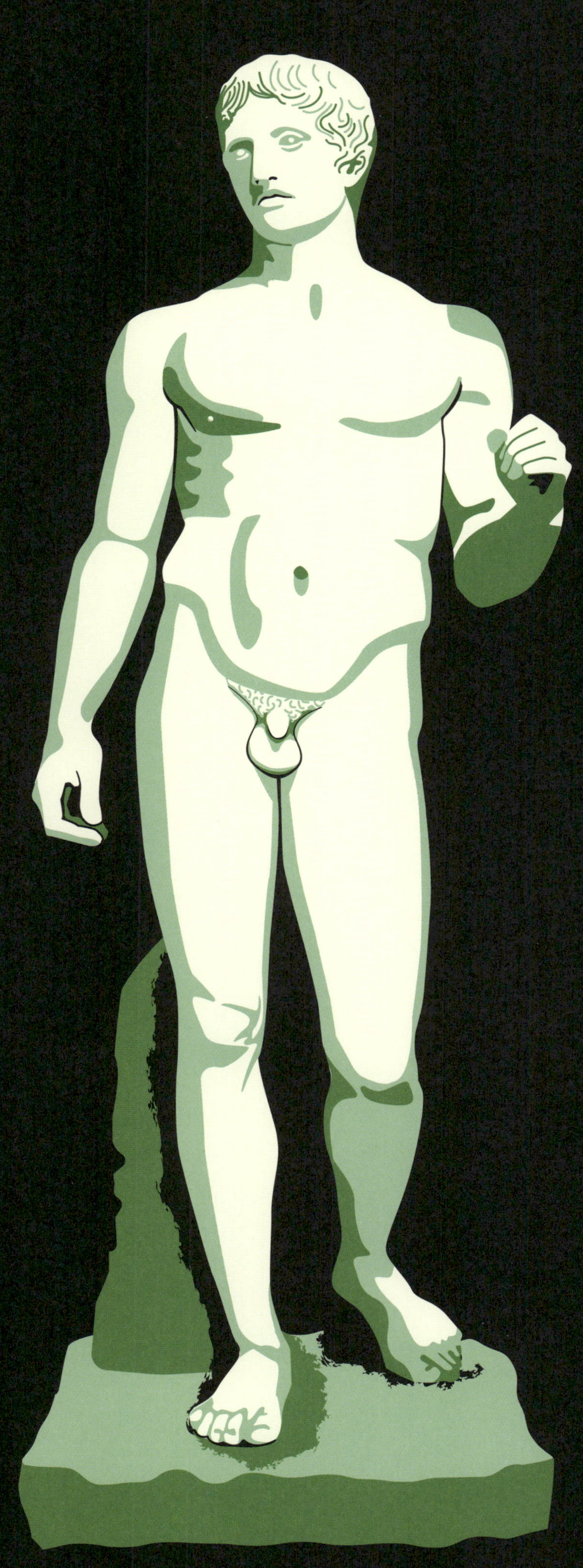

DORYPHOROS

The original "Doryphoros", created in the fifth century BCE by Polykleitos, was lost in ancient times but we know what it looked like from marble copies. The sculpture's pose and proportions may make him look like a real man but this is an idealized body, not an authentic one.

THE WALKING MAN (L'HOMME QUI MARCHE)

Giacometti moulded this sculpture in clay before it was cast in bronze in the 1960s. Although this man is life-sized, he certainly doesn't look real like "Doryphoros" does. However, the sense of movement from his pose still seems to bring him to life.

PORTRAITS

Put simply, a portrait is a representation of someone. But portraits don't just depict a likeness; they can send a message, capture the character of the person portrayed or even reveal what they might be thinking.

WHY MIGHT YOU have a portrait made? Portraits have played an important role in showing status and power for thousands of years. They have been used as reminders of loved ones who are absent, given as gifts and collected by families through the generations to record their history. They have been created to record marriages and to immortalize the dead on their tombs. Some of our greatest artists specialized in portraiture and the most famous were highly sought after. Portraits were once only created for the wealthy or those close to an artist, but with the invention of photography they have become accessible to all. Some of the earliest portraits depict rulers and are found on coins; this was a way to spread their image far and wide and demonstrate they were in charge. Augustus, the first Roman emperor, used his portrait in sculpture and coins to spread the message of his power, rather like a logo.

Augustus's face is now one of the most recognized faces from the ancient world because hundreds of sculptures of him have been discovered from all over his former empire.

Elizabeth I also took control of her image through portraits great and small. She didn't always sit for portraits in person and had "patterns" for how she was to be depicted. The English artist Nicholas Hilliard was a celebrated painter of tiny portraits called miniatures and created several of the queen. Their small size meant that miniatures could be easily carried around and worn by loyal subjects.

Portraits don't just focus on individuals. In 1768 King George III founded the Royal Academy of Arts in London, a place for teaching and exhibiting. The German artist Johann Zoffany, famous for creating lively, jam-packed portraits of large groups, painted the academy's founding members gathered together for a life drawing class with two male models. Amongst the artists captured on the canvas are Joshua Reynolds, who was the academy's president and one of the greatest portrait painters of the time, and Zoffany himself. Two founders, however, have been excluded – Mary Moser and Angelica Kauffmann. They would not have been allowed in the room as women were banned from attending such classes. Instead, Zoffany has painted their portraits hanging on the wall. Being forbidden from formally studying the whole human body meant that female artists couldn't gain sufficient experience of painting expressive postures, and many were therefore forced into painting portraits.

Like the people they depict, portraits come in all shapes and sizes, from tiny paintings to larger-than-life sculptures. Today portraits are still everywhere – from gallery walls to coins in your pocket.

VAN EYCK

Jan van Eyck's 1434 "Arnolfini Portrait" depicts a couple holding hands in a lavish room wearing expensive clothes. On the wall the artist has written "Jan van Eyck was here" and below it a mirror reflects two figures back at us, one of whom is waving. Has he painted his way into the scene?

PORTRAITS OF AUGUSTUS

Everyone in the Roman Empire would recognize Augustus. He died in 14 CE at the age of 75 but his portrait didn't age over the forty years he was in power.

1. The Meroë Head was discovered in Sudan. It was removed from a larger-than-life sized bronze sculpture of Augustus.
2. This coin showing Augustus dates to between 7 and 8 BCE and was probably made in France.
3. A stone carved with a relief image is known as a cameo. This relief portrait of Augustus has been carved into its different coloured layers.
4. This type of sculpture is called a bust. This one of Augustus looking youthful was actually made later in his reign.
5. Caesar, written on this coin, was a title given to emperors. It came from Augustus's adopted father, the dictator Julius Caesar.
6. Known as the "Prima Porta", this statue shows Augustus dressed as a general and was found in the ruins of his wife's villa.

PAINTING A SELF-PORTRAIT

Today, anyone can take a selfie, but historically self-portraits were the work of artists. They have been made for practice, experiments and to show off their skills.

Albrecht Dürer
This celebrated Renaissance artist produced a number of self-portraits. He drew studies of his face and included himself in paintings created for clients, a bit like a signature. Other artists had done the same but Dürer went further – he was one of the first artists to paint just himself. In this self-portrait from 1500 he seems to be presenting himself as a Christ like figure, perhaps to show his status as an artist and creator.

Sofonisba Anguissola
Italian artist Anguissola was one of the first internationally famous female painters of the Renaissance, going on to paint at the Spanish court of King Philip II. Self-portraits were a way to promote herself early in her career but she kept painting herself into her seventies. This image, with rubies and pearls in her hair, may have been painted after she arrived in Spain.

Farrukh Beg
Farrukh Beg was one of the most revered artists at the Mughal court, and his work includes an illustration for the story of Emperor Akbar's life, the *Akbarnama*. This painting, dating to around 1615, is signed by him and is thought to be his self-portrait. It was part of an album belonging to Akbar's grandson Shah Jahan.

Artemisia Gentileschi
Gentileschi was one of the greatest artists of the seventeenth century. In this self-portrait from around 1615–17, she has painted herself as Saint Catherine who was tortured on a wheel. It is perhaps a hint at the fact that the resilient Gentileschi was herself tortured during a court case when she was just seventeen. In another possible self-portrait she depicted herself as painting in human form.

Rembrandt van Rijn
Rembrandt van Rijn was the master of the self-portrait, and over the course of forty years he created around ninety self-portraits in painting, drawing and etching, playing with costumes and expressions. As he grew older, he looked hard at his ageing face, as he has done in this painting from 1665. His expression seems to reveal the hardships of his life.

Thomas Gainsborough
Gainsborough was one of the top English portrait painters of the eighteenth century, and his subjects were wealthy and fashionable. This self-portrait is from 1759. Gainsborough preferred painting landscapes but nature played a role in some of his most famous portraits – countryside conversation pieces showing groups in casual poses.

Self-portraits make artists look hard at themselves, whatever the motive, and they allow us to admire an artist's work whilst also giving us an insight into their mind – or at least what they want us to see.

Francisco de Goya
Spanish artist Goya is famous for capturing who his subjects were as people, not just how they looked (meaning his portraits weren't always flattering!). This self-portrait from 1815 captures a sense of his fragility. After suffering a mysterious illness which left him deaf, a dark romanticism seeped into Goya's work. His portrait painting continued but he began to create sinister works depicting real and imagined horrors.

Julien Hudson
Hudson was the son of a freewoman of colour and a white Englishman. He was born in New Orleans in 1811 and would go on to study in Paris. This 1839 painting is thought to be a self-portrait, which would make it the first and only surviving self-portrait by an African American artist from this time. Its small size may reflect his training in miniature painting.

Vincent Van Gogh
The Dutch artist Van Gogh created over forty self-portraits in the space of ten years, often using himself as a model because he couldn't afford to employ one. His paintings of himself show his development as an artist. This portrait was painted in 1889, a year after he cut part of his ear off, and the same year he admitted himself to an asylum and painted "Starry Night".

John Singer Sargent
Singer Sargent painted portraits of presidents – and portraits which caused a stir. This 1906 self-portrait was to be hung in the corridor of the Uffizi Gallery in Florence alongside those by some of the most famous European artists in history. As one of the first Americans to be invited to join their ranks, his appearance shows how seriously he took the honour.

Egon Schiele
The Austrian artist Schiele died in 1918 at the age of twenty-eight from influenza, but in his short life he created thousands of artworks. Amongst them are a great number of self-portraits, including this one from 1910. He used self-portraits a bit like mind experiments, depicting himself in contorted poses pulling all sorts of faces using a whole host of colours.

Amedeo Modigliani
This Italian painter and sculptor is famous for his unique style. He was influenced by African masks and experimented with lengthening faces in sculptures. Transferring this style to his paintings, he elongated his subjects' faces and necks and gave them blank eyes. We can see this employed in this self-portrait painted in 1919.

COURT ARTISTS

Rulers and royals have employed artists at their courts for centuries. Both could benefit from the relationship – a famous artist could bring prestige to a court, and the artist had guaranteed work from a powerful patron which might just shape a country's fate.

ARTISTS HAVE BEEN incredibly important for figures of power since ancient times. In the fourth century BCE, Alexander the Great conquered a vast empire, which stretched from Greece to India. He employed some of the greatest artists of the time, and they alone were allowed to make his portraits.

Court artists didn't just depict their royal employers – they did much more.

In the sixteenth century, the great artist Hans Holbein the Younger was court artist to King Henry VIII. Holbein created decorations for Henry's palaces and designs for elaborate metalwork, such as daggers, but he is most famous for his portraits. As well as painting the king, his role was to produce portraits of potential wives. Exchanging portraits was an important part of negotiating royal marriages, which were necessary for producing an heir and also created important alliances between countries. Future spouses might live far away and not meet until the wedding itself, so portraits were the only way to see what each other looked like. After the death of Henry's third wife, Jane Seymour, Henry was on the lookout for a new bride and Holbein was sent to paint possible prospects. Holbein's portrait of Anne of Cleves, who was from Germany, helped Henry decide to marry her and the wedding took place in January 1540. But the marriage lasted less than a year! The story goes that when Anne arrived, she didn't look much like her portrait.

A court painter's duties could go even beyond painting. Peter Paul Rubens was the court painter to Archduke Albert and Archduchess Isabella, who governed part of the Netherlands for the king of Spain. After Albert died, Rubens acted as a diplomat for Isabella, representing her in foreign lands, and was so good at this role that it took him to England on behalf of the Spanish king, Philip IV, to negotiate peace with Charles I. Whilst Rubens was there, Charles commissioned him to decorate the ceiling of the Banqueting House at the Palace of Whitehall in London – one of the last things Charles would have seen before he was beheaded there in 1649.

VAN DYCK

Charles I's own court painter was the Flemish artist Anthony Van Dyck, who had once been Rubens's assistant. Van Dyck created famously flattering portraits of the king, including several of him on horseback designed to show his majesty. His paintings went on to influence portraiture for centuries.

From 1623, the court of Philip IV was home to one of the great artists of all time – Diego Velázquez. In his role as the king's painter he created the 1656 masterpiece "Las Meninas" ("Maids of Honour"). It is a huge painting, with characters including Philip's daughter, Margarita, and Velázquez himself standing at an enormous canvas. Much more complex than a group portrait, its lasting mysteries mean that this court painting isn't just for the royals – we can enjoy it too.

"LAS MENINAS"

This painting is both a portrait and a puzzle. What is happening? Why is Velázquez in this royal portrait painting and what is he working on?

Reflected in the mirror are the faces of King Philip and Queen Mariana. Is that who most of the figures are looking at?

Although the royals might be in the room, most agree the reflection is actually of Velázquez's canvas. Has he cleverly shown us his painting?

Velázquez's clues tell us he isn't painting the princess. So why is everyone here? Perhaps she is visiting him and her parents have joined her – she can see them but we can't. Including himself might show his high status as the king's painter and his ambition – the symbol on his chest belongs to an order of knights he desperately wanted to be part of.

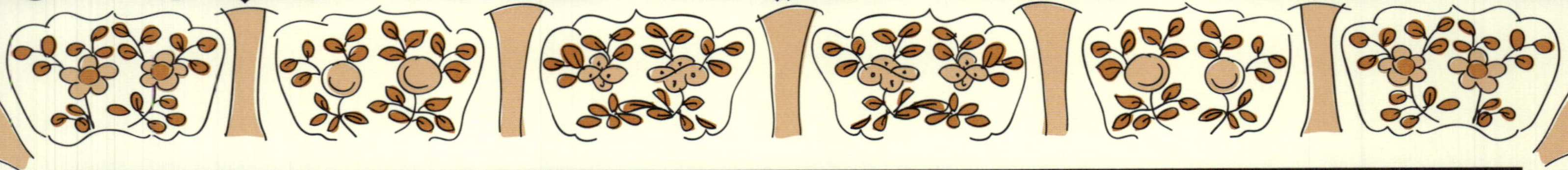

STILL LIFE

With subjects such as dead fish, cheese and apples, you might not think that still life sounds like the most exciting genre of art. In fact, it was once considered to be the lowest form of painting. However, paintings of inanimate objects have been popular for thousands of years and are not only intricate and experimental but can carry hidden messages.

THE HISTORY OF this style of painting stretches back to the ancient world. Food was painted on the walls of ancient Egyptian tombs as an offering to the dead, and in the fifth century BCE, as legend has it, a Greek artist called Zeuxis painted a bunch of grapes which looked so real that birds flew down from the sky to try to eat them. But it wasn't until the seventeenth century that still life became a genre in its own right. Still-life painting was especially popular in the Netherlands and the name derives from the Dutch word *stilleven*. Amongst the earliest pioneers was a Flemish artist called Clara Peeters, one of the few women who painted professionally at that time. She created some of the first still lifes which feature hunted animals, and painted what might be the first ever still life of a fish. Many of her impressively realistic works feature food, and are called banquet pieces.

Van Gogh painted some of the most well-known still lifes – his seven vases of sunflowers are famous the world over.

Still lifes don't just include things you can eat. Rachel Ruysch was an expert in depicting flowers, and her vivid paintings portray assortments of blooms in incredible detail. Picked flowers in still-life paintings sometimes have a deeper meaning. Pieter Claesz painted several still lifes which are known as *vanitas* paintings, including one from 1625 of a freshly picked flower, a skull, a watch and a candle which has nearly burnt out. These objects are all reminders to the viewer that life is fragile and fleeting.

In more recent history, still-life painting has been used to challenge tradition. In the second half of the nineteenth century, the humble apple played a vital role in the still-life paintings of Paul Cézanne. He once said he would "astonish Paris with an apple" – and he did. They were one of his favourite subjects in his paintings, which broke free from traditional laws of perspective and experimented with shape and colour. In the twentieth century, Georgia O'Keeffe took the genre in a new direction and is perhaps most famous for her huge paintings of magnified flowers. These brave and bold works, which took such a close look at traditional subjects, were thoroughly modern. Throughout history, artists have used still lifes to make us look more carefully.

POMPEII

In 79 CE a volcano in Italy called Vesuvius erupted, raining ash and stones from the sky and burying the Roman city of Pompeii. Around 2,000 people are thought to have died in the disaster and many more fled, abandoning their homes. The eruption preserved the city, giving us a glimpse into Roman life – and art. Pompeii is rich with paintings and many villas left behind are decorated with paintings of food.

"STILL LIFE WITH CHEESES, ALMONDS AND PRETZELS"

Although she is one of the great innovators of still-life painting, Clara Peeters herself is a bit of a mystery. Very little information about her survives but her paintings give us some hints about her life.

In around 1612–15 she painted "Still Life with Cheeses, Almonds and Pretzels" and it looks good enough to eat (if you like cheese, that is). This image of the meal laid out on a stone table gives us some clues to Peeters's identity.

Tucked behind the plate of cheese is this jug with a shiny pewter lid. Looking out at us from a reflection in the lid is Peeters herself in a tiny self-portrait. By putting herself in her painting, she wants us to recognize her and her talent.

In the seventeenth century, it was the custom to take your own cutlery to a dinner party. If we look carefully at the handle of the silver knife placed at the edge of the table, besides two pretzels, we can see Clara Peeters's name written along the edge. The same knife appears in five other paintings of hers, and is the type of gift you'd receive upon getting married. A marking on the blade shows it was made in the city of Antwerp and suggests this might have been where she lived.

This painting doesn't just reveal clues about Peeters, it also tells us something about the world she and her clients lived in. The almonds, raisins and figs are on a blue and white porcelain plate from China. This type of porcelain, known as *kraak*, was highly sought after and collected by royalty. Behind it is a gilded Venetian glass cup. These are expensive objects which may have been designed to appeal to clients who wanted to show off their wealth or good taste.

LIGHT IN ART

Light is a vital element in art. It makes golden mosaics glitter and stained glass shine. In painting, artists imitate the effects of light to bring their works to life.

ARTISTS CONTRAST LIGHT and shadow in their paintings to create a feeling of three dimensions and add drama. This is called chiaroscuro, combining the Italian words for light (*chiaro*) and dark (*oscuro*). We can see the effects of chiaroscuro if we look at two paintings created by Leonardo da Vinci between 1483 and 1508. Both paintings are called "The Virgin of the Rocks" and they depict the same subject: the Virgin Mary in a rocky landscape with an angel and two children, Jesus and St John the Baptist. Although the scenes are nearly identical, the later version has a stronger contrast between light and shadow on Mary's face and neck which makes the image feel more real. We could almost forget Mary is painted on a flat surface.

When we talk about light in art we also have to talk about the absence of light.

Around a hundred years later during a period known as the Baroque, the artist Michelangelo Merisi da Caravaggio took chiaroscuro a step further. We can see the drama created by Caravaggio's contrasts between light and dark in a painting created around 1609–10 which also depicts St John the Baptist. In "Salome receives the Head of John the Baptist", John has been beheaded and an executioner holds out his head by his hair. Cast half in shadow, it almost feels like it is being thrust out of the painting. The head is being presented to Salome, the woman who requested this cruel death, but her illuminated face turns away from the gruesome sight. Not everyone approved of Caravaggio's use of darkness, but it influenced many artists who came after him.

REMBRANDT

In Amsterdam, Rembrandt van Rijn used light to create drama and capture emotion in his paintings and etchings. In "The Artist's Studio", a drawing from 1659, we can see how Rembrandt manipulated natural light. A model is sitting ready to be painted in his studio, bright in the light from the window. The lower set of shutters is closed and a cloth hangs above to reflect light down onto her.

Beyond Italy, masters of light could be found that same century in the Netherlands – Rembrandt van Rijn and Johannes Vermeer. One hundred years after them, J. M. W. Turner was born. He became one of Britain's greatest artists, famous for his stormy paintings and use of strong contrasts and colour to create dramatic light on his canvases. It wasn't for nothing that he was called the "painter of light".

In the twenty-first century, artistic obsession with light has continued in new ways. British artist Martin Creed won a major art prize for his controversial piece "Work No. 227: The lights going on and off", in which the lights in a room do just that. In "Infinity Mirrored Room – The Souls of Millions of Light Years Away" the Japanese artist Yayoi Kusama hung different coloured lights in a room covered from floor to ceiling in mirrors. Their reflections seem to spread all around you into endless space. Their methods might change, but artists will always use light to add new dimensions to their work.

"GIRL WITH A PEARL EARRING"

Vermeer painted "Girl with a Pearl Earring" around 1665; it has become one of his most famous paintings.

MAKING A PRINT

Prints are some of our most influential artworks because countless copies can be made of a single image. The same picture can be seen or owned by people across the world.

MAKING A PRINT can be as simple as pressing one surface to another, but there are a number of ways to create the initial image and transfer it onto paper. Woodblock printing is one of the oldest methods and was invented in China in the seventh century CE. From the seventeenth to the mid-nineteenth century, some of the world's greatest woodblock prints were created in Japan. These prints are called *ukiyo-e*, meaning "pictures of the floating world". Depicting actors, beautiful women, landscapes and scenes from everyday city life, they were intended to show the fleeting nature of life's pleasures.

Prints could be bought for as little as the price of a bowl of noodles, so almost anyone could own one.

Katsushika Hokusai was one of the greatest *ukiyo-e* artists. Born in 1760, by the age of six he had started drawing. Although we know him now as Hokusai, during his seventy-year career he changed his name over thirty times – once after he was struck by lightning! Hokusai was an all-rounder, and in addition to some 3,000 colour prints he also created thousands of paintings and illustrated hundreds of books. Experts predict that in total he created over 30,000 works.

"THE GREAT WAVE"

This is one in a series of views of Mount Fuji created by Hokusai in the 1830s, in which the sacred volcano is seen from under bridges, across rivers, through a barrel and towering over a storm. The views were hugely admired and between 5,000 and 8,000 images of "The Great Wave" were printed. Hokusai's work reached across the world and we can see his impact on the work of Van Gogh and Monet.

Hokusai's print "Under the Wave off Kanagawa", or "The Great Wave", is one of the most famous images in the world. A vivid blue wave with a white foaming crest dominates the scene and hangs threateningly over three boats and their crews which can just be spotted on the stormy sea. In the background is Mount Fuji, tiny in comparison with the wave which looms over it. The distant mountain shows Hokusai's clever use of perspective, which was inspired by European artworks.

In Europe, meanwhile, printing only really took off from the late fourteenth century when paper became more readily available. Albrecht Dürer was a master of printing, and one of his works shows just how influential a printed image could be. In the early 1500s an Indian rhinoceros was sent as a gift to the king of Portugal. It was over a thousand years since a rhinoceros had been seen in Europe, and news of this mysterious beast soon spread. Dürer drew one based purely on descriptions and sketches – meaning it doesn't actually look like a real rhino. It's covered in armour and has an extra horn above its shoulder! Dürer's drawing was turned into a print and became so well known that for the next two hundred years it was how many European illustrators depicted rhinoceroses. The power of print! Printing continues to be one of our most important inventions – you wouldn't be reading this book without it.

UKIYO-E WOODBLOCK PRINTING

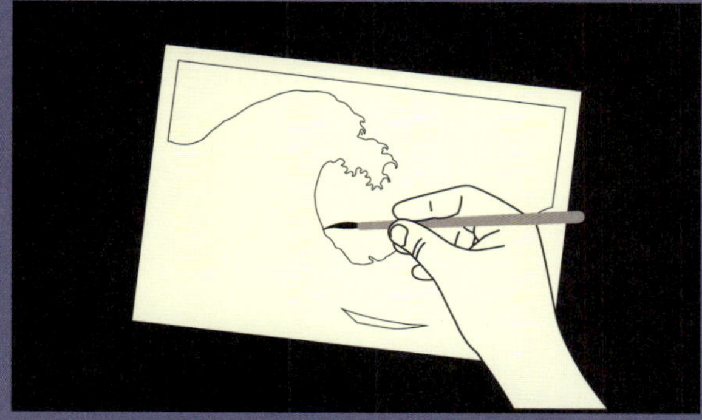

1. The artist creates the design for the print on very fine paper using ink and a brush.

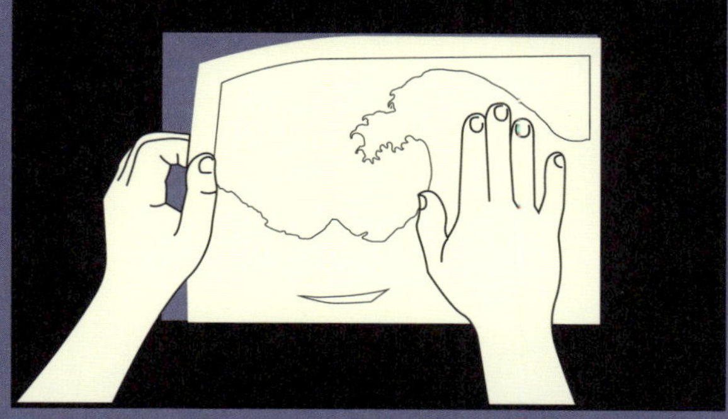

2. The design is then given to the carver who makes the woodblocks. The design is reversed and carefully pasted onto a block of wood.

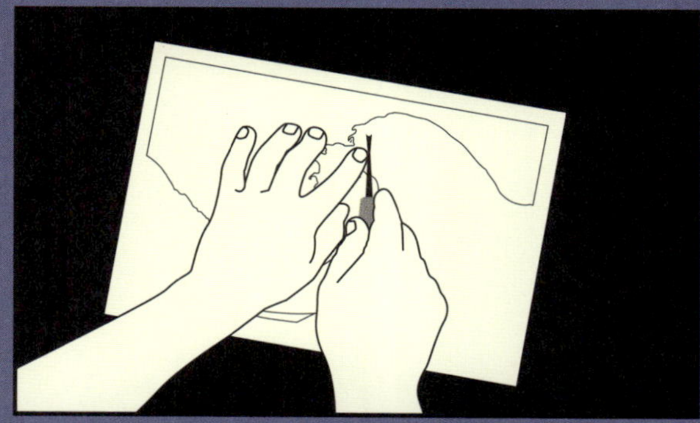

3. The block-cutter uses a knife to cut around the design into the woodblock.

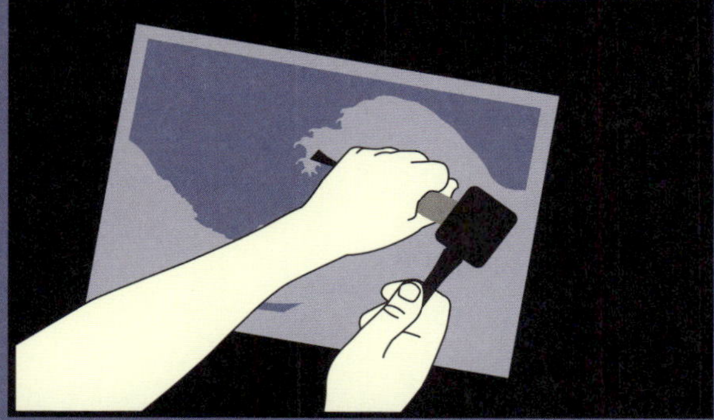

4. The excess wood between the lines and around the design is removed using different types of chisel.

5. This is the key block and it prints the outline of the image. Prints from this block will be used to make a block for each different colour.

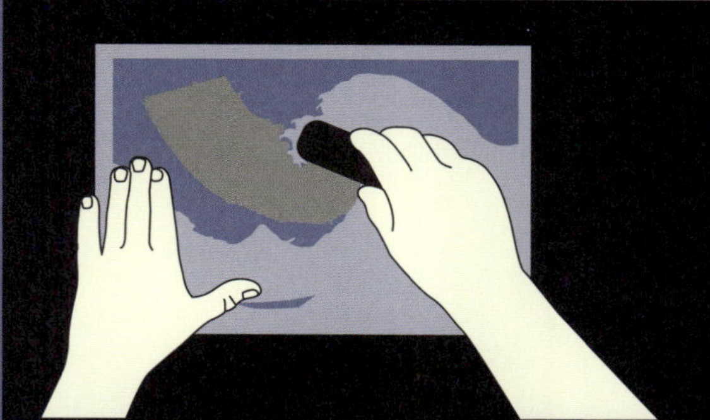

6. The printer now takes over. Colour is painted onto the block using a horsehair brush. The key block is the first to be printed.

7. Next, the paper is placed on the block. Each block has a notch called a *kento* cut into one corner to act as a guide for the paper so that everything is aligned.

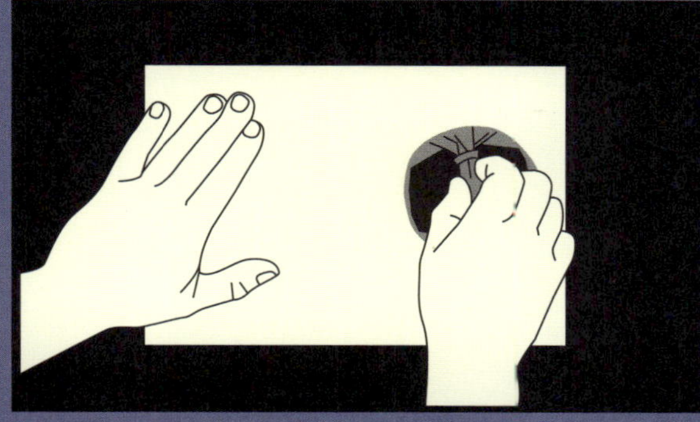

8. The printer rubs the paper with a type of pad called a *baren* to transfer the colour onto it from the block.

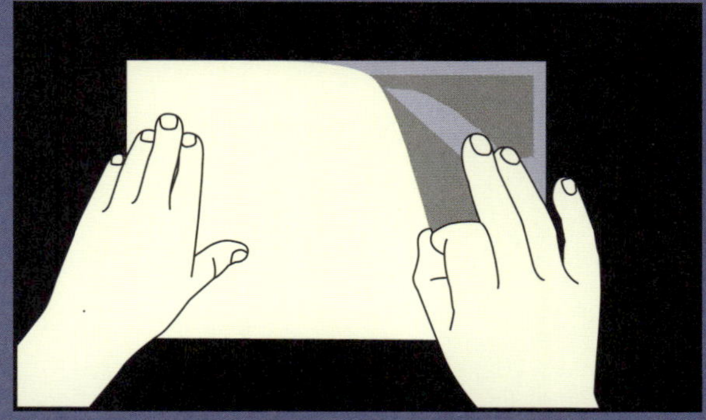

9. The paper is removed and the printing process is repeated for each colour, building up the image block by block.

"The Great Wave" is made up of yellow, black, grey and different shades of blue, and a very faint trace of pink can be seen in some versions. If we look at some of the individual colours which go into making the majestic wave, we can see how the parts come together to make the final masterpiece. If the colours didn't align properly then the image would be ruined.

LANDSCAPES

Landscape painting takes nature as its main subject. For thousands of years, different cultures around the world have depicted landscapes in their art and they often reveal far more than we might think at first glance.

THE GREEKS AND ROMANS painted scenes from nature on their walls but after ancient times in Europe, it wasn't until the 1500s that landscapes stopped just being in the background of paintings and took their place as a genre in their own right.

Landscape painting was looked down on as a low-ranking type of painting for centuries because humans were not the main subject.

In China, however, landscape painting had developed into an important genre by the tenth century. Chinese landscapes are called *shanshui* paintings, meaning "mountain and water", and they usually depict idealized or imagined landscapes which carry deeper meanings. During the Northern Song dynasty (960–1127), landscape became one of the highest art forms and a way to convey philosophical and political ideas, such as representing the correct order of the state. Guo Xi was one of the greatest landscape artists from this period and painted for the Song court. The central peak in his monumental work "Early Spring", painted in ink on a silk scroll in 1072, may represent imperial importance but people have also found spirituality and emotion in his work.

When landscape painting *did* take off in Europe, some of the greatest artworks were created by artists from the Netherlands. One of them was Pieter Bruegel the Elder, who in 1565 produced a series of paintings on wooden panels based on the seasons. At the time, there were considered to be six seasons and Bruegel's six paintings combine depictions of the changing landscape with highly detailed scenes from everyday life. In "Hunters in the Snow", a group of dogs follow three hunters as they return to their village. In the distance we can see people ice-skating and playing games on frozen lakes, and beyond them are towering snowy mountains. You almost feel cold looking at it. Bruegel imagined this landscape but his work shows how connected people were with nature and its power.

RUISDAEL

In the 1670s Ruisdael painted "View of Haarlem with Bleaching Grounds", a depiction of his home town, in which the most dominating element is actually the vast sky. It takes up well over half of the canvas and shows that it wasn't just the land that was important in the landscape genre. The sun shines from behind the clouds, leaving some parts of the ground illuminated and others in shadow.

The seventeenth century in the Netherlands has become known as the Dutch Golden Age of painting; during this period, landscape painting really put itself on the map. One of the greatest landscape artists from this time was Jacob van Ruisdael, who was an inspiration to one of Britain's most famous landscape painters – John Constable.

Constable's paintings mostly depict the countryside of his home county of Suffolk and capture the feel of the places he knew so well. The greatest landscapes have the power to say as much about people, including their artists, as they do about nature.

"THE HAY WAIN"

"The Hay Wain" (1821) is perhaps John Constable's most famous work and, at over two metres square, it was designed to grab our attention. The view depicted is about a mile away from where Constable was born. In fact, the pool of water in the scene is the millpond used to power the mill run by Constable's family for almost one hundred years. Constable actually painted the scene in his London studio, but he had been drawing the area for nearly twenty years and used a handful of sketches he had made ten years before as a reference. From the full-scale sketch he did in preparation for the finished painting we can see he intended to include a horse with a rider. The finished painting didn't sell in England and ended up being sent to Paris, where Constable won a medal for his work.

Constable is famous for his skies, which he thought played a vital role in landscapes. He sketched scientific studies of clouds and used them to create different moods in his work.

The wagon is empty because it is making its way over to the group of haymakers we can see working in the background with their scythes. Another wagon has already been loaded with a huge pile of hay and we can just make out a figure standing on top of it all.

Constable had a colourful palette and used vibrant greens at a time when paintings were made to look brown in the manner of old prestigious works. His brushwork also broke with tradition – rather than using smooth strokes, he dabs and scrapes his paint onto the canvas.

ROMANTICISM

The eighteenth century was a time of turmoil. As it came to an end, a new era of art emerged called Romanticism. Instead of a common style or look, Romantic art was characterized by capturing feeling, imagination and nature.

THE AMERICAN REVOLUTION freed the United States from British control in the eighteenth century, the Industrial Revolution transformed the way people lived and worked, and the bloody French Revolution began a period of terror and spread war throughout Europe. Although this was a time of change and disorder, the key values had been order and reason, and artists were inspired by the ancient art of Greece and Rome. The Romantics reacted against this, looking inside themselves to emotion and imagination, and outside to the power of nature. In doing so, they didn't shy away from the ugly, the horrifying and the painful.

Romantic landscape artists found emotion in the uncontrollable power of nature and took the genre to new heights. J. M. W. Turner and his fellow Englishman John Constable were two of the great Romantic landscape artists. We can see the impact of the Industrial Revolution in their work as Turner evoked a rapidly changing world by combining the forces of nature with new technology, whilst Constable painted nostalgic countryside scenes.

Inner worlds provided inspiration for many Romantics, and the English artist William Blake used his to fuel poetry, painting and print. His work is original and unique, and often a product of the changing world around him, his religious beliefs and moral ideas. From a young age, Blake had visions, and these, along with his vivid imagination, played a vital role in his creations. His famous painting, "The Ghost of a Flea", was inspired by a vision he had in around 1819–20. He saw the ghost of a flea, which told him that all fleas held the souls of bloodthirsty men. Blake paints his flea carrying a cup to use for drinking blood.

During his career, Blake was called "an unfortunate lunatic", but he is now remembered as a visionary.

The Romantics set the course for the artists who came after them to explore their imaginations and express feeling in their art. Their powerful works still stir our emotions today.

"THE RAFT OF THE MEDUSA"

The great French Romantic painter Théodore Géricault used real-life horrors as inspiration. His enormous painting "The Raft of the Medusa" depicts the aftermath of a famous shipwreck in 1816. One hundred and fifty poor souls were left adrift on a raft and when help finally came after thirteen days at sea, only fifteen had survived. To stay alive, they had resorted to cannibalism. The painting is inspired by the accounts of survivors, who also modelled for the scene. Géricault's raft is surrounded by enormous waves and littered with dead bodies. Amongst the handful of despairing survivors, a single man attempts to wave to a ship disappearing over the horizon. This type of work is called a history painting (the highest genre), which traditionally depicted biblical stories, myths or historical events – not a recent disaster and people driven to unspeakable lengths.

"WANDERER ABOVE THE SEA OF FOG"

THE ORIGINS OF MODERN ART

When we talk about the origins of modern art, they might not sound very modern. Although people disagree over exactly when it began, modern art is usually seen as starting around the middle of the 1800s. It saw a flourishing of new art styles which changed the way art was made and can be seen as a series of movements – many ending with "ism" – including Impressionism, Post-Impressionism, Cubism and Surrealism. At its beginning were some of the greatest artists experimenting with new techniques, new ideas and new subjects. They laid the foundations for generations of artists who came after them.

In 1863 the famous official art exhibition in Paris, the Salon, rejected Édouard Manet's painting "Luncheon on the Grass". When it did go on show, it scandalized its audience. A naked woman sitting with two men was shocking – and the fact that their clothes were from the present day made it even worse. This scene, which feels boldly flat due to its unrealistic perspective, is considered to be one of the earliest works of modern art, and Manet would become associated with the beginnings of Impressionism – one of the first modern art movements.

Georges Seurat was a Neo-Impressionist and took a more scientific approach to his paintings. His masterpiece is "A Sunday on La Grande Jatte – 1884", a huge painting depicting Parisians enjoying a leisurely Sunday in a park by a river. When you look closely at the painting, you can see it is made up of tiny contrasting coloured dabs. This technique is called pointillism (from the French word for "dot"), and when viewed from further away these dots blend together to make the colours more luminous.

The Dutch artist Vincent Van Gogh came to Paris in 1886 and became inspired by the Impressionists and Neo-Impressionists. His colours brightened and his brushstrokes loosened, creating an emotionally expressive style. "Starry Night" was painted in 1889 whilst he was in an asylum and was inspired by the view from his window. He added to the scene from his own imagination – the village was not visible from his room and the moon and stars glow with an unnatural intensity. His expressive style would have a huge impact on modern artists, especially the Expressionists and the Fauves.

Paul Cézanne's paintings were shown in Impressionist exhibitions in the 1870s but he turned away from the movement, wanting to create art which felt more solid. His explorations of depth, form and colour made him one of the most important Post-Impressionists. Around 1887 Cézanne painted "Montagne Sainte-Victoire with Large Pine", capturing the landscape near his home town in the South of France by building up forms using bright colours. His work paved the way for Cubism and abstract art.

Norwegian artist Edvard Munch was a Symbolist, which meant he explored ideas rather than reality. In "The Scream", painted in 1893, a terrified figure with a gaping mouth stands in a landscape with a sky painted in waves of red and orange. Munch wrote that one evening whilst out walking he felt a scream tearing through nature – this was his inspiration, and the painting captures how he felt. Munch had a great influence on Expressionism, which looked beyond the outside world to what was inside us.

Paul Gauguin was inspired by Impressionism but moved on to Symbolism, which he made his own with large areas of unnatural colour. Gauguin spent time in Brittany in northern France and there he was inspired to paint "Vision of the Sermon (Jacob Wrestling with the Angel)" in 1888. It is one of Gauguin's most original works, depicting a group of praying women in traditional dress who have just heard a religious speech based on the biblical story. Beyond them is their vision of Jacob and the angel, painted against a background of vivid red.

Austrian artist Gustav Klimt was the first president of the Vienna Secession (meaning "breakaway"), a group founded in Vienna in 1897 which rejected old-fashioned approaches to art. Despite this, Klimt looked to the past and in his 1907 painting "Adele Bloch-Bauer I" we can see him take inspiration from golden Byzantine mosaics and use it to dissolve her body into patterns.

Henri Rousseau taught himself to paint, and his work is seen as an early example of what is called naïve art. His paintings show his lack of knowledge of techniques like perspective, but that was seen as evidence of true expression. Other modern artists were great fans of his work, including Pablo Picasso. "Surprised!", painted in 1891, is one of over twenty jungle paintings but Rousseau never left France during his lifetime; instead this scene is created from his imagination and draws inspiration from houseplants, Botanical Gardens, a zoo and stuffed animals.

IMPRESSIONISM

Today, Impressionism is one of the most well-known movements in art, but in the nineteenth century it was a revolution. Artists broke from tradition to paint scenes of modern life and the momentary effects of light in vibrant colours using clearly visible brushstrokes.

IN 1874, A GROUP OF ARTISTS called the Anonymous Society of Painters, Sculptors, Printmakers, etc. came together to hold an exhibition in Paris which would go down in history. We know them as the Impressionists. The name of the movement came from one of the paintings in the exhibition, "Impression, Sunrise" by Claude Monet – but it was not meant as a compliment. A reviewer used the word "impression" to criticize the work for looking sketchy and unfinished. Alongside Monet were artists who would later go on to be celebrated around the world – Auguste Renoir, Edgar Degas and Berthe Morisot. What brought them together was the fact that they were rebels. Indeed, what had led to the exhibition in the first place was a rejection of the artists' work by the Salon – the most prestigious exhibition in France, which had strict rules about art.

The Impressionist artists' controversial brushwork makes their paintings instantly recognizable. We can clearly see the strokes and dabs of the paintbrush, which are loose, rapid and feel spontaneous. The focus wasn't on perspective or depicting forms clearly; instead, the goal of Impressionists was to capture the fleeting effects of light in a single moment; to express the way we actually see and feel. Colour was vital. They didn't limit themselves to neutral tones and instead used bright, brilliant paint, even in the shadows. They used tubes containing premixed paints and without the mess of mixing their own colours, artists could take their canvases outside, allowing them to work directly from their subjects and observe the changing light and colours.

Impressionists used a ground breaking invention: the paint tube.

The Impressionists' subjects were thoroughly modern, normal people doing everyday things. Historically, this was certainly not thought to be important enough for art, which was supposed to show ancient myths and stories from history. Instead, these paintings showed people in theatres, cafes and bars, walking through parks or along the river.

But bars and cafes were off limits to female Impressionists like Mary Cassatt, the only American to exhibit with the Impressionists. Cassatt hated conventional art and her paintings are mostly of modern women at home, or in respectable settings, such as a theatre box.

MONET

Monet continued to explore light and colour after the last Impressionist exhibition, painting the same subjects at different times of day. He is famous for his near 200 pictures of waterlilies, but he also painted over 20 poplar trees.

Impressionism came to an end in the 1890s and although the movement was short-lived, its impact spread through Europe and the US, paving the way for new styles and great artists, including Van Gogh. Impressionism had broken the rules and caused controversy – and in doing so changed the course of art.

MONET PAINTING EN PLEIN AIR

The Impressionists' habit of painting outside is called painting *en plein air.* In 1870 Monet went on holiday to the French coast with his wife, Camille, and their son, Jean, and painted a series of *en plein air* works including this scene of Camille sitting with another woman called "The Beach at Trouville". We know Monet painted this outside, because if you look closely you will find grains of sand which blew onto his wet paint!

PHOTOGRAPHY

A photograph is an image made when a material that is sensitive to light is exposed to it. Artists seized upon this invention and have used it to transform the way art is made.

IN 1833, WHILST on honeymoon in Italy, an Englishman called William Henry Fox Talbot tried his hand at drawing using a device called a camera lucida. This used a glass prism attached to a metal arm which allowed him to look at a view whilst reflecting it onto his paper, so he could trace it. But Talbot was sorely disappointed with his drawing in comparison to the reflection and became determined to find a way to capture these images created by light. In France others had been developing methods of fixing images to metal but in 1839 Talbot revealed a process using paper. And so began the route to modern photography.

Julia Margaret Cameron was a pioneer, receiving her first camera in 1863 and quickly going from amateur to innovator.

One of the most popular initial uses for photography was portraiture. Julia Margaret Cameron photographed influential Victorians as well as her family, dressing them up as literary and biblical characters. Some laughed at her use of atmospheric light and soft focus, thinking photographers should aim for sharp pictures, but others recognized her talent.

Within sixty years of the invention of photography, almost anyone could own a camera. In 1916 a teenager called Ansel Adams was given his first camera and went on to become one of the greatest landscape photographers of the twentieth century. He is most famous for his pictures of Yosemite National Park in California; he wanted to capture how these vast mountains made him feel.

Since the nineteenth century, photographers have used their cameras to document the reality of human tragedy. During the Great Depression, Dorothea Lange worked for the US government and her images raised awareness of people's struggles. In 1936 she photographed a poverty-stricken mother with her children who had been surviving on vegetables they found in frozen fields. During the Second World War the photographer Lee Miller was with Allied forces as they discovered the atrocities of the Nazi concentration camps.

WAR PHOTOGRAPHY

The American Civil War was one of the first wars to be captured on camera. At that stage, the exposure time was too long for action shots, but we do have staged photos post-battle.

Before the war, Miller had worked with the artist Man Ray in Paris. Man Ray had a vital role in Dada and Surrealism and his photographs play with reality. Some of his most famous images were created by placing objects like faces and combs onto photographic paper and exposing them to light. These acted like stencils and created groundbreaking images which he called rayographs after himself. The process was similar to Talbot's early experiments.

Since its invention, photography has transformed the whole world around us. It has had an impact upon everything from science to fashion and has been used to record major historical moments. Today, everywhere we look, we see photos.

"BOULEVARD DU TEMPLE"

This image of a quiet street in Paris is one of the most important photographs ever taken. It was captured in 1838 by Louis-Jacques-Mandé Daguerre using a method he had developed called the daguerreotype process. It was the presentation of this to the public in 1839 that made William Henry Fox Talbot race to reveal his own method. Daguerre used a copper plate coated with silver which he made sensitive to light using iodine. The image was captured by exposing the plate to light using a lens, which took some time, and then mercury vapours and a salt solution were used to develop and fix the image. The daguerreotype created images with amazing detail, like this one, but the length of time required for exposure meant that the people in this street moved too quickly to be captured. Except, that is, for this bootblack polishing his client's shoes. These two were in the same place long enough to make history as the first people ever to be photographed.

CUBISM

Cubism was one of the biggest revolutions in the history of art. Rather than trying to recreate how things appeared in real life, it was a new way of depicting the world by looking at multiple angles and breaking subjects into different parts.

FOR CENTURIES, ARTISTS had used techniques like perspective to capture reality – but the Cubists had a new approach. Its inventors, a Frenchman called Georges Braque and a Spaniard called Pablo Picasso met for the first time in 1907. It was Braque who created the first work to be called Cubist. In 1908 he submitted a series of landscapes he had painted in L'Estaque in the South of France to an exhibition. These paintings, which use overlapping flat painted areas to depict their subjects, were inspired by techniques used by Paul Cézanne, who had a huge influence on Cubism. Every one of Braque's paintings was rejected from the exhibition and his painting "Houses at L'Estaque" was criticized for looking as though it was made up of "little cubes". The name Cubism was born.

Cubists emphasized that their paintings were flat objects.

PICASSO

Picasso's journey towards Cubism took him outside Europe and back in time. He was fascinated by African art along with art from ancient Iberia (Spain and Portugal today). These influences came together in his 1907 painting "Les Demoiselles d'Avignon", which depicts five nude women with flat and distorted pink bodies. Two of them have faces which look like African masks. This work exploded the old traditions of using perspective and depicting lifelike bodies. No one had seen anything like it before, and people found it extremely shocking.

Picasso and Braque worked together closely, painting Cubist still lifes and human figures. It's often hard to tell their work apart. In 1910 both artists depicted women with mandolins (a guitar-like instrument). In Braque's painting, the woman and her mandolin are like a patchwork of different interlocking shapes and forms. We can make out the hole in the mandolin, the woman's hand on the neck of the instrument, and some features of her face, but it's difficult to see where her body might end and the background begins.

A new phase in Cubism began in 1912 and it was then that Picasso invented collage, which means "to glue" in French. In 1914 Braque created another image of a mandolin, this time combining drawing, newspaper and corrugated cardboard. In the same year, Picasso made a sculpture of a guitar from sheet metal. Assembling ordinary materials rather than carving or moulding forms in bronze or stone was groundbreaking at the time.

In 1914 the First World War broke out and Braque was called up to join the fighting. After the war, he and Picasso never regained the same friendship, but together they had torn up the rule book and changed art for ever. Their imagination had inspired artists such as Juan Gris to create Cubist works and would go on to influence major movements and experiments like Surrealism and abstraction.

THE TWO PHASES OF CUBISM

Cubism developed in two phases. In the first phase, known as Analytical Cubism, Picasso and Braque looked at their subjects from multiple perspectives and broke them down into fragments which they fused together in their paintings. They used neutral browns and greys in order not to distract from their compositions. Breaking down their subjects showed they were three-dimensional and that the painting itself was flat.

A second stage called Synthetic Cubism emerged in 1912. Picasso and Braque began to add materials from the world around them, like newspaper, to their artworks to build up their subjects. These artworks are much flatter and more colourful.

ABSTRACT ART

In the early twentieth century, artists started to create paintings which don't look like anything we might recognize. They do not depict people or objects, and in fact, they rejected representation altogether. This is called abstract art.

SO, WHAT WERE THEY PAINTING? In Moscow in 1915 an artist called Kazimir Malevich exhibited a groundbreaking new painting: a single black square on a white background. It might sound simple, but that is part of its power. For Malevich, colour and shape were supreme, and this painting was a new beginning for art.

"Black Square" shows that a painting does not need to be rooted in reality. An artistic revolution was happening.

Malevich wasn't the only Russian at the front line of abstract art. Wassily Kandinsky started out as a lawyer but in 1896, at the age of thirty, he began to study art in Munich and became one of the great abstract innovators of the early twentieth century. The Dutch artist Piet Mondrian's journey to abstract painting began with his vibrant, unnaturally colourful traditional Dutch landscapes, along with seascapes which he broke into horizontal and vertical lines. From 1919 he made grids which featured only certain colours – red, blue, yellow, black, white and grey. He poured thought and feeling into these, experimenting with where to position the fields of colour and black lines to create the perfect painting. His final painting is called "Victory Boogie Woogie", referring to his love of boogie-woogie music, which began when he came to New York in 1940 to escape the Second World War.

KANDINSKY

Kandinsky painted traditional scenes for years before exploring abstract art, and in his early abstract paintings we still find hints of reality which have been reduced to lines and colours. He placed great importance on how line and colour were arranged and felt this could create an emotional response in the viewer, like music.

Kandinsky, Malevich and Mondrian may be three of the most famous names in early abstract art, but in Sweden an artist called Hilma af Klint was creating abstract artworks years before any of them. Between 1906 and 1915 she created 193 artworks which together are called "Paintings for the Temple". Like other abstract artists, af Klint was interested in the spiritual, creating many of her paintings whilst she believed she was in contact with spirits. However, she was also influenced by science, and some of her works have imagery which resembles cells. When she died in 1944 at the age of eighty-one, she left instructions that her paintings must not be exhibited for twenty years. In the end, it took forty years for this pioneer to begin to receive the recognition she deserves.

Abstract art took hold of painting and artists continued to experiment. Abstract Expressionists explored emotion and expression and the most famous, Jackson Pollock, almost danced around his huge canvases as he poured and dripped on paint to make his evocative works. In fact, abstraction would become so normal that artists would rebel against it!

MONDRIAN'S JOURNEY TO ABSTRACTION

1.

2.

3.

4.

5.

6.

1. The Red Tree, 1908
2. The Flowering Apple Tree, 1912
3. Composition No. II, 1913
4. Composition No. 10 Pier and Ocean, 1915
5. Composition C, 1920
6. Composition No. II, with Red and Blue, 1929
7. Victory Boogie-Woogie, 1942–44

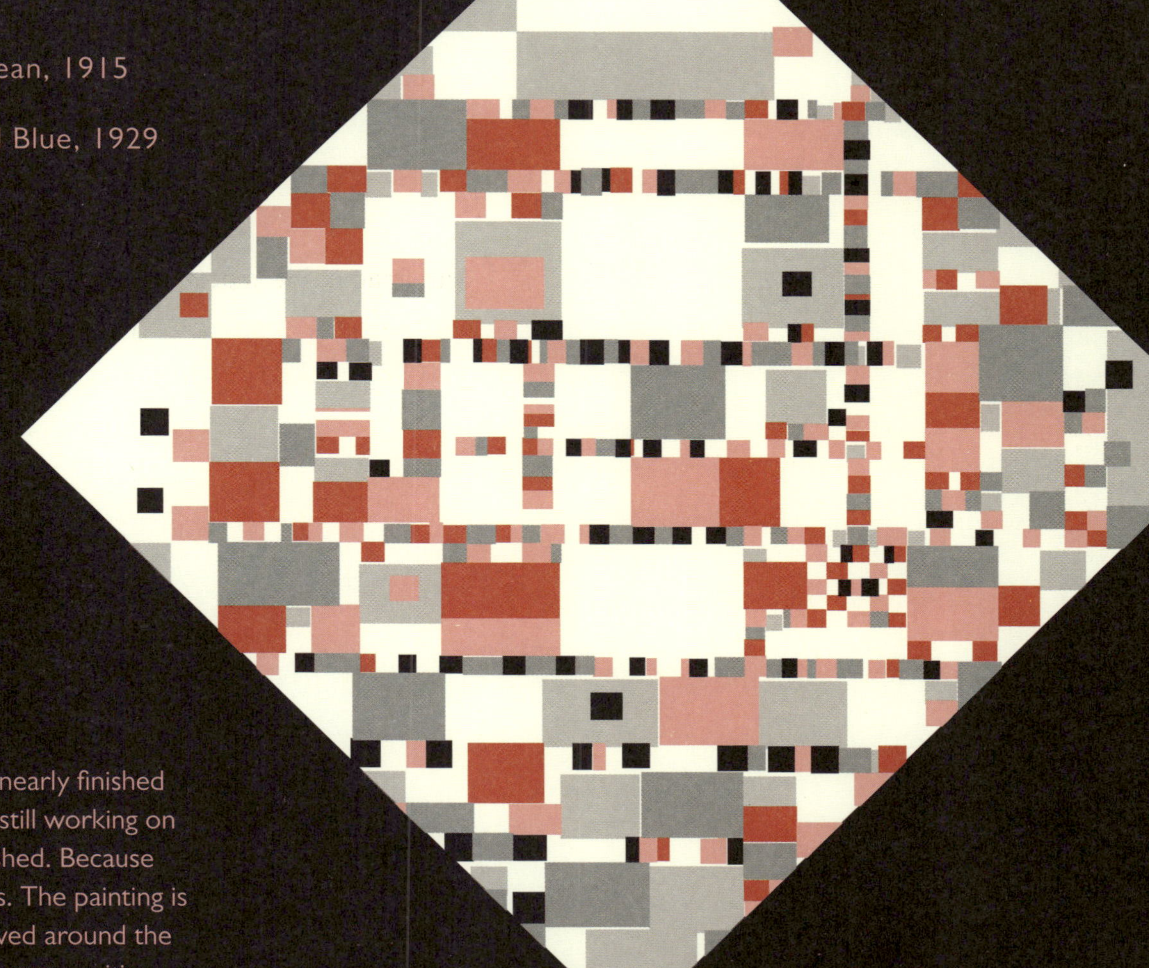
7.

Mondrian said that "Victory Boogie-Woogie" was nearly finished several times – but then kept on working. He was still working on it when he died in 1944 and it has remained unfinished. Because of that we can see evidence of Mondrian's process. The painting is littered with pieces of coloured tape which he moved around the canvas to experiment with different colours in different positions.

SURREALISM

In 1924 a weird and wonderful new type of art was born: Surrealism. Rather than looking at the world around them, Surrealist artists expressed what they saw in their dreams, their imagination and their subconscious – the inaccessible part of your mind which affects your behaviour.

ONE OF THE WAYS Surrealists tapped into their subconscious was by experimenting with automatic drawing. French artist André Masson, one of the early Surrealists, started with no plan or subject: he just let his pen move across the page. From his tangles of lines emerged figures. Salvador Dalí's work included Surrealist objects made through bringing together unexpected and unconnected items. In 1936 he made four lobster telephones for the country house of an English poet. Dalí wasn't the only artist who created Surrealist objects. In the same year, at the age of twenty-two, Meret Oppenheim created one of the most famous: "Object". The idea came to her after a lunch she had with Pablo Picasso and Dora Maar. Picasso, noticing Oppenheim's fur-trimmed bracelets, said that almost anything could be covered in fur. She replied "even this cup and saucer". Soon after, she put her suggestion into action, buying a cup, saucer and spoon from a department store and covering them in the fur of a Chinese gazelle. The fur totally transforms these normal objects, making the commonplace bizarre, shocking or even disturbing. Fur is luxurious and soft to touch – but not so nice to put in your mouth, which is what we'd have to do if we used this cup and spoon. Oppenheim's jarring "Object" confuses our senses and muddles our assumptions with its combination of the wild and the civilized.

Artist Dora Maar created Surrealist photos, including a hand coming out of a shell.

René Magritte was another Surrealist who brought together different objects in his work, often combining words with images. He is perhaps most famous for an oil painting he created in 1929 called "The Treachery of Images". Magritte depicted a realistic-looking smoking pipe and underneath it he wrote *Ceci n'est pas une pipe* which translates as "This is not a pipe". He's right, of course: it's a picture of a pipe, not the real thing. But we recognize the image instantly as a pipe. The message of the writing is in conflict with the image. Which wins? Surrealism still has us guessing what is real and what isn't.

DALI

Salvador Dalí, a Surrealist who created not just art but food, fashion and even worked with Walt Disney, often described his works as "hand-painted dream photographs". His unreal images are strikingly realistic. In "The Persistence of Memory", a coastal landscape is littered with strange objects. Soft watches, inspired by melting cheese, stretch and hang over different elements in the painting, including a tree branch and a mysterious creature which seems to have a single eye. One watch is face down and a group of ants, which Dalí hated passionately, crawl on its back. But the painting didn't come entirely from his imagination – the coastline is inspired by his memory of Spain, where he grew up.

A SURREAL WORLD

"Object"
Meret Oppenheim, 1936

POLITICAL ART

Art can be used to express emotion, capture a moment and explore the way we look at the world. The twentieth century saw an explosion in what art can be, with some trying to control it and use it as a tool for their own ends.

IN 1917 A REVOLUTION broke out in Russia and everything was turned upside down. The royal family were removed and the Bolsheviks, a communist group who wanted everyone to be equal, took charge. It was the start of something new, and at first, there was freedom for artists to experiment and create exciting new work. But that soon changed, and after Joseph Stalin came to power, a type of art called Socialist Realism became the official style. Those who did not follow it were in danger. The style was old-fashioned, promoted communist values and showed a bright future. Paintings depicted farm workers, happy families, heroic figures and powerful leaders. "Letter from the Front", a painting by Alexander Laktionov, depicted a cheery family on a sunny day and received a prize from Stalin. The family are reading a letter from their father fighting at the front during the Second World War; none of the horrors or hardships of war are captured. That is because this so-called realism was not the reality. Under Stalin's rule people lived in fear, starvation swept Russia, millions died and millions more were imprisoned in forced labour camps.

Formidable leaders and regimes have used art to assert and reinforce their power for centuries.

The early twentieth century was a time of great change in Germany too. Artists explored bold new styles, which were challenged when Adolf Hitler came to power in 1933. The Nazis despised modern art and removed over 16,000 artworks from museums. In 1937 they held an exhibition called *Entartete Kunst*, meaning "Degenerate Art", which was designed to show the public the evils of modern art. Over 650 works of art in styles including Cubism and Expressionism were put on show. Wassily Kandinsky, Pablo Picasso and Henri Matisse were amongst the 112 artists whose work was included. The labels ridiculed the artworks and artists, with newspapers describing the works as horrifying and "trainloads of dirt". Jewish artists were heavily blamed for modernism, even though only six of the artists included were Jewish. Huge crowds visited the exhibition, which went on tour across Germany, and after it finished, many artworks were burnt or sold to raise money for the Nazis. At the same time as the Degenerate Art exhibition, another was held showing art that the Nazis approved of. The Nazi style of art developed to be much like that of the Socialist Realism of Russia. Again, we see happy families and heroic figures, promoting the regime.

FLEEING RUSSIA

Malevich, creator of the abstract masterpiece "Black Square", began to paint his own versions of peasants and farming scenes in bright colours, but many other artists fled the country.

The twentieth century may have been a time of fantastic artistic development but it was also a century which saw art used for dark and terrible purposes.

"THE TOWER OF BLUE HORSES"

"The Tower of Blue Horses", painted in 1913 by the German Expressionist Franz Marc, went on display in the Degenerate Art exhibition. Marc is famous for painting animals, which he considered to be spiritual, in bright colours. The painting was withdrawn after a group of army officers protested because Marc had died fighting for Germany in the First World War. Afterwards, it was taken by Hitler's deputy Hermann Göring and its location is still unknown.

POP ART

In the 1950s, British and American artists began to make art inspired by everyday images and objects. This was Pop art. Comics, burgers, celebrities – this movement was inspired by what was popular, but although the subjects were familiar, this art was radical.

IN 1956 THE ARTIST Richard Hamilton created a collage using American magazines called "Just what is it that makes today's homes so different, so appealing?" It was one of the first artworks to include the word "pop", which is written on a lollipop held by a bodybuilder who is standing in a room filled with everyday items such as a TV and a Hoover. Hamilton pioneered this new type of art, which he thought should have certain qualities, like being witty and low cost. Over in America Abstract Expressionism had taken hold of art but Pop artists turned away from this inward-looking style, depicting what they saw around them, exactly as they saw it. Popular culture and objects made and sold in massive quantities now took centre stage, from cars to groceries; adverts to film stars.

The word "pop" was first used in Britain, where artists began to take inspiration from popular culture.

In 1962 an art gallery lined a shelf with thirty-two cans of soup as if it were a supermarket. They were works of art, each can hand-painted on to a canvas by the artist Andy Warhol. The series is called "Campbell's Soup Cans" and there is one painting for every flavour the Campbell company produced. These cans of soup are now some of the most recognizable images of Pop art, and Andy Warhol became the most famous artist of the Pop art movement. He had started out as a commercial illustrator, drawing for magazines and adverts, and when Pop art emerged in New York in the 1960s, he was quick to become part of it. As well as soup cans, he depicted Coca-Cola bottles, dollar bills and Mickey Mouse!

Processes of mass production, that is producing large numbers of the same object, influenced the techniques Pop artists used to make their works. The American artist Roy Lichtenstein's artworks were inspired by comic books, including speech bubbles and sound effects like "BLAM" and "POW". He used dots to mimic the industrial way of printing images used in comic books and newspapers. Mass production also appealed to Warhol, whose studio was even called The Factory. Warhol was also inspired by commercial printing and took a process used to make adverts called silk-screen printing to create many of his most famous works.

Pop art had a huge impact, springing up around the world as far as Japan, Russia and Brazil, and continues to inspire artists. Will you ever look at a can of soup in the same way again?

MARILYN MONROE

Warhol was obsessed with celebrities, and the actress Marilyn Monroe was the subject of one of his first screen prints in 1962, the year she died. Warhol wasn't the only artist who put Marilyn in their art. Across the Atlantic in the following year, British artist Pauline Boty painted the Hollywood star in "The Only Blonde in the World".

LICHTENSTEIN'S "BRUSHSTROKES"

Lichtenstein's inspiration for "Brushstrokes" came from a comic book story about an artist tormented by a man in one of his paintings. To silence him, the artist paints over the man's face. Lichtenstein has adapted and enlarged part of the scene which shows the painting after its destruction.

Lichtenstein created this painting in 1965 as part of a series. The image feels like it has been made industrially because of the flatness of the brushwork and use of dots. This is a play on the idea that brushstrokes are expressive.

Lichtenstein is famous for his use of dots. They are called Ben-Day dots and were used in industrial printing to create different colours and tones. They look much bigger on his canvases than they do in their usual settings as he blows up his subjects. At first he painted his dots by hand, but he went on to develop a way of painting them using stencils.

For Sheila and Dorothy H.H.

For Hogan and Tamara J.B.

First published 2020 by Walker Studio, an imprint of Walker Books Ltd
87 Vauxhall Walk, London SE11 5HJ

This book has been typeset in Gill Sans and Superclarendon

Printed and bound in China

British Library Cataloguing in Publication Date: a catalogue record for this book is available from the British Library.

ISBN 978-1-4063-9389-7

www.walkerstudio.com
www.walker.co.uk